SUPER
RICH

SUPER RICH

A GUIDE TO HAVING IT ALL

RUSSELL SIMMONS

WITH CHRIS MORROW

GOTHAM BOOKS

GOTHAM BOOKS
Published by Penguin Group (USA) Inc.
375 Hudson Street, New York, New York 10014, U.S.A.
Penguin Group (Canada), 90 Eglinton Avenue East, Suite 700, Toronto, Ontario M4P 2Y3, Canada
(a division of Pearson Penguin Canada Inc.); Penguin Books Ltd, 80 Strand, London WC2R 0RL,
England; Penguin Ireland, 25 St Stephen's Green, Dublin 2, Ireland (a division of Penguin Books
Ltd); Penguin Group (Australia), 250 Camberwell Road, Camberwell, Victoria 3124, Australia
(a division of Pearson Australia Group Pty Ltd); Penguin Books India Pvt Ltd, 11 Community Centre,
Panchsheel Park, New Delhi—110 017, India; Penguin Group (NZ), 67 Apollo Drive, Rosedale,
North Shore 0632, New Zealand (a division of Pearson New Zealand Ltd); Penguin Books (South
Africa) (Pty) Ltd, 24 Sturdee Avenue, Rosebank, Johannesburg 2196, South Africa

Penguin Books Ltd, Registered Offices: 80 Strand, London WC2R 0RL, England

Published by Gotham Books, a member of Penguin Group (USA) Inc.

First printing, January 2011
1   3   5   7   9   10   8   6   4   2

Gotham Books and the skyscraper logo are trademarks of Penguin Group (USA) Inc.

LIBRARY OF CONGRESS CATALOGING-IN-PUBLICATION DATA
Simmons, Russell.
Super rich : a guide to having it all / Russell Simmons, with Chris Morrow.
p.   cm.
ISBN 978-1-592-40587-9 (hbk.)
1. Self-realization.   2. Conduct of life.   3. Attitude (Psychology)   4. Spiritual life.
I. Morrow, Chris.   II. Title.
BF637.S4S54854   2011
204'.4—dc22
2010040619

Printed in the United States of America
Set in Bembo with Avant Garde Gothic
Designed by Sabrina Bowers

To my two first ladies,
Ming Lee and Aoki Lee

CONTENTS

REDEFINING RICH   1

ATTRACTING THE WORLD   15

SUCCEEDING THROUGH STILLNESS   31

THE WORK THAT PRAYS   65

BEING A BUSINESS YOGI   91

BE REBORN EVERY DAY   109

BUILDING BRIDGES   131

ACCEPTANCE IS THE ANSWER   153

MATERIAL BURDEN   175

NOT TOO HOLY   189

SUPER RICH

REDEFINING

RICH

Life finds its purpose and fulfillment in the
expansion of happiness.
—MAHARISHI MAHESH YOGI

I'd like to start this book with a few words about my last one. Though its title might have suggested otherwise, *Do You!* was written for *me*.

Not in the selfish ways that can motivate some—for money, the ego boost of seeing your words in print, or receiving accolades in the press. Instead, I wrote *Do You!* primarily as a cleansing process.

As those familiar with my story already know, I come from Hollis, Queens, a lower-middle-class African-American community where spiritual direction primarily came from either the Christian Church or The Nation of Islam, worldly success was reflected by the car you drove, physical prowess was mea-

sured by how well you shot a jumper, and everyone's diet re-
volved around meat.

Yet after embracing the physical practice of yoga roughly
fifteen years ago, and my subsequent exposure to spiritual texts
like the Yoga Sutras, the Bhagavad Gita, and the Hatha Yoga
Pradipika, I realized that there were paths I could take that
might prove more beneficial for me than those I was expected
to follow. Paths that still ran parallel to the Judeo-Christian
tradition of my upbringing, but that would allow me to become
more connected to my higher self and as a result less harmful in
my relationship with the world.

As I became more committed to practicing yoga, meditation,
and philanthropy, and removing meat from my diet, I could feel
myself becoming a better businessman, a better leader, a better
father, and a better giver—in short a better human being.

On the eve of my fiftieth birthday, I felt an urge to unbur-
den myself of some of those principles I'd learned over the years
by sharing them with the world. I had already discussed these
beliefs with my friends and family (some of whom would probably even say ad nauseam) and promoted them in interviews
over the years, but I had never attempted to disseminate them
in an organized and digestible manner.

I described that urge as "selfish" because while I certainly
wanted to help people transform their lives, I was equally motivated by the belief that "downloading" all this information
out of my heart and into a book would make *me* a better person.
By writing a book about these principles, I believed I would be
able to glean a better understanding of them in the process.

Outside of my own development, I honestly didn't suspect
that the book would have much of an impact. The rap on me,
no pun intended, was that I was the guy who helped put hip-
hop music on the map by co-founding Def Jam Records and

introducing artists like Run DMC, The Beastie Boys, Public Enemy, LL Cool J, Ludacris, DMX, and Jay-Z to mainstream America. Who found subsequent success through ventures like *Def Comedy Jam*, *Def Poetry Jam*, Phat Farm clothing, and *Run's House*. Who over time earned the title of "the Godfather of Hip-Hop," as well as one I'm a little more comfortable with, "Uncle Rush."

And while those are accomplishments that I'll always humbly cherish, I didn't feel they necessarily set the stage for me to write a book where yoga, philanthropy, and God played a major role. Sure, people might turn to me for concrete advice on how to get a record deal or launch a clothing line, but would they view me as someone who could help them get in touch with their higher selves? Would they see the connection between my worldly successes and my spiritual practices?

The answer, to my eternal gratitude, was yes. Despite my reservations, *Do You!* connected with a larger audience than I ever expected it would, earning great reviews and even becoming a *New York Times* best seller. Yet while those worldly accomplishments were nice for my ego, my greatest validation came from the reactions I heard on the street. If I went to see a movie, it always seemed like when the film was over, a couple of people would come up to me and say, "Hey, Russell, I just wanted to thank you for *Do You!* It really changed my life." The book seemed to resonate with so many folks, from so many different walks of life.

There was the young black kid who approached me at one of our Hip-Hop Action Network Summits and told me that *Do You!* had motivated him to go to college instead of staying on the streets and hustling like the rest of his friends.

There was an older Russian Jewish socialite, someone that I'd see at "society" events around New York City, who came up to me at a party and told me that while she had suffered from a very dark depression for many years, *Do You!* finally helped her find some light in her life.

There was Brother Mohammad, who stood outside my office in a bow tie and overcoat every day for a week, waiting for a chance to pitch me a business idea. When we finally spoke, the first thing he did was pull out a worn copy of *Do You!* and show me all the passages that he'd underlined, concepts he said had helped him find the confidence to pursue his dreams.

There was the heroin addict around the corner from my office who told me *Do You!* was the transformational tool that helped him finally kick his habit for good. And I could go on and on.

The reaction to *Do You!* was perhaps the most meaningful I've received for any project I've shared with the world. I personally run five philanthropic organizations in addition to supporting several organizations I'm not directly associated with. I've also spent years working to help put an end to senseless drug laws, the abuse of animals, and every kind of "ism" and "phobia," efforts that I like to think have had a positive impact. But none of those efforts have been a greater gift than *Do You!*'s ability to lift people's consciousness by even just one degree. None of those efforts provided me with a comparable platform from which I could share the gift of consciousness and help people awaken to their true potential. Inspired to take full advantage of that platform, I decided to pen a follow-up to *Do You!* that went deeper into the spiritual practices that have become more and more important to me as I've gotten older.

I realize that given *Do You!*'s emphasis on spiritual principles, some of you might be surprised by the title of this book. So before we go any further, let me clarify why I decided to call it *Super Rich*. The journey that I'm promoting in this book, despite what the title might seem to suggest, is not one that's going to culminate in a mansion with a luxury car in the driveway. What I'm encouraging you to strive for, and really what I'm seeking myself, is something much greater. So rather than any state of material abundance, *Super Rich* actually refers to living in a state of consciousness where you're able to see the miracles of life unfolding in front of you all the time.

It's a state where your connection to your higher self is so strong that you'll be able to recognize that there's no difference between being broke and being a millionaire, between a beautiful sunset and a terrible thunderstorm, between a newborn baby and the corpse of an old man. It's a state where you'll be able to appreciate that your entire experience as a human being is blissful and sublime.

And as a result of achieving this state, you'll understand that you don't need money or toys to be happy. That's right, when you're Super Rich you'll be able to see that happiness is actually a state of needing nothing.

What I'm suggesting might sound radical, but it really ain't nothin' new. In actuality, all the faiths have a term for this blissful state—for example, Christians call it "Christ Consciousness," yogis call it "*Samadhi*," and Buddhists call it "Nirvana." But let's be real: If I wrote a book with Christ Consciousness or *Samadhi* in the title, most of you would have had a hard time taking it seriously. So I decided to go with *Super Rich,* following a conversation I had with my ex-wife, Kimora Lee. After I shared the concept for the book with her one day, her response was "Oooh. You're trying to teach them how to be super rich!"

Some of you might be shaking your head right now and thinking, "What's going on here? I thought this book was going to be about making some money!?" But if that's the reaction you're having, please, please bear with me.

I understand what I'm promoting can be a difficult concept to grasp at first. So difficult, in fact, that even my own brother Reverend Run (you might know him as the patriarch of MTV's *Run's House* as well as from Run DMC), who is a direct disciple of the famous prosperity preacher Reverend Ike, didn't accept it at first.

I learned this when Run sauntered into my office one day while I was working on the book and plopped himself down on my couch.

"So, what are you going to call this book?" he asked me.

"*Super Rich*!" I responded. "Which is the state of needing nothing."

"What?!" he asked skeptically. "People don't want to hear that being 'super rich' means needing nothing when they're trying to keep up with their car notes, or pay their mortgage, or find a new job! When someone spends twenty-five dollars for a book from 'Mr. Hip-Hop Mogul,' they're expecting to learn how to get paid!"

"But that's exactly how you do get paid!" I shot back. "Accepting that you don't need things to be happy is exactly how you can develop the faith and courage to get that house with a bathroom that looks like a spa in the Four Seasons. Needing nothing is how you're actually going to get everything! When you can give your full attention to serving the world, instead of worrying about the world giving you things, you will be so attractive that people will literally start throwing money at your feet. That might fly in the face of what some people were expecting, but I'm sorry, I can't be like some of these folks out here who claim to know some secret way to make a lot of money that doesn't involve having a sweet, generous, and compassionate spirit."

"Relax, Russell, nobody is saying you should tell people

how to make money in a way that is disconnected from their higher self," replied my brother. "But you might want to remember a piece of wisdom my mentor Bishop Jordan taught me when I was studying the Bible: that Jesus had two sermons."

"What does that have to do with *Super Rich*?"

"Well, Jesus understood that it was helpful to use two different sermons while spreading his word: One sermon was the parables he shared with the masses, stories that were tuned into people's day-to-day lives. Jesus knew that if he got too spiritually high and mighty on the regular folk whose biggest concern was putting food on their tables and getting the Romans their taxes on time, then most of them would have just tuned him out. So instead he brought them into his flock by addressing their worldly needs first. But when Jesus was alone with his disciples, he would go very deep into his mystical trip. Those dudes had already abandoned all their worldly concerns, so they were more than ready for Jesus's purely spiritual rap."

When Run told me that, it rang a bell in my head and awoke me to the possibilities of taking a similar approach in these pages. So in this book, I'm going to hit you with what are essentially two sermons. The first is that in order to be truly happy and realize the full potential of your life, you must always try to move toward enlightenment. A state where you are fully conscious of and connected to the world around you and the God inside of you. Where you walk through life with a smile on your face and give without expectation.

The second is that the road to enlightenment is paved with gold! This is because when you're truly conscious and give without expectation, you'll be so attractive to the world that every toy, every material possession, will find its way to you.

But here's the thing: The more enlightened you become, the less interest you'll have in those toys. You might like to hold them for a second, but you won't be interested in *holding on* to them. Because your connection to God will remind you that you don't *need* any of it!

It may not be what you're used to hearing, but I promise you will be happier and more successful if you can break free of the constraints of feeling like you need money and toys. While the toys can be a lot of fun, I've learned firsthand that real richness lies in simply being happy with what you have. Whether it's a lot, a little, or nothing at all. When you have a rich spirit, you're already rich. You won't need anything else. When you can be happy and comfortable in every position, or situation, that you encounter in life, then all the obstacles that you perceive as standing between you and happiness will gradually disappear. It will become easier to fill your life with friendship, laughter, love, and yes, for those who still desire it, money.

Yet while I believe a rich spirit is ultimately all any of us needs, don't get it twisted: I'm not telling anyone that they should stop searching for worldly success. Instead, I'm simply encouraging anyone who feels like they need more than what they have to cleanse themselves of what I call a "poverty mind-set." Stop suffering needlessly because you believe that you have been "shut out" from making it. You might feel shut out because of your race, your economic situation, your sex, your sexuality, your social standing, or even your physical appearance. No matter what it stems from, when you have a poverty mind-set you're going to believe that the object that will make you happy is always just outside your grasp.

How many times have we convinced ourselves that once we get a certain job, a certain car or a certain house, or even lose a certain amount of pounds, then everything in our lives will

Super Rich Errata

Page 10, fourth paragraph:

I'll say it again, I'm just asking that you *hold on* to them.

should read:

I'll say it again, I'm just asking that you *don't hold on* to them.

simply fall into place? That once those toys appear, then we'll be "The Man" or "The Woman"? Yet the truth is that there's no check, or car or house or perfect weight that you need to wait on in order to be happy. You're already "The Man" or "The Woman."

No matter what the world tells you, happiness isn't something that is determined by exterior forces like toys, race, or class. Instead, happiness is something that each of us is born with inside our hearts. As human beings, it's our most basic birthright. It's the most beautiful gift we're given in life, one that can never be taken away from us.

But while happiness is inside of us, unfortunately we often can't hear it because it's drowned out by the clutter created by the toys. The goal is to clear out that clutter and quiet that noise. And this book will help you find ways to do that.

The burden of not connecting with your God-given happiness is the heaviest load you can carry in life. Heavier than unrequited love, poverty, or even loss. When we fail to connect with our gift, we suffer. Sometimes terribly. Your belly may be full, but if you can't hear your happiness, you will still feel empty inside.

So as you move through this book, I want to encourage you to try to redefine what *rich* means to you. If you read these pages while clinging to the belief that richness can only be measured through the toys you accumulate (or the "results" of your work), then I'm afraid that you're going to miss out on a lot of what I have to share.

If, however, you can accept that the toys and the money will only be the by-products, instead of the aim, of your journey toward enlightenment, then you will have positioned yourself to be truly rich. To realize your greatest potential.

RICH IS RELATIVE

Before I go any further, I want to address a reaction some of you might be having to hearing me say that the money and toys should have no bearing on your happiness:

"That's easy for the rich guy to say."

It's a response I often hear whenever I start talking about concepts like "redefining rich" and "needing nothing." I hear it on the streets, from audiences, on Twitter, and even from other rich guys!

I can certainly understand the sentiment. Why should you listen to me when I'm writing this book up in my penthouse surrounded by all my toys? The answer, as I'll lay out in greater detail in subsequent chapters, is that just because I'm suggesting that you need nothing doesn't mean that I'm asking you to forgo any toy that I've enjoyed. I'm not telling you that you shouldn't enjoy driving a Rolls-Royce or watching a movie on a fifty-inch HD television. Those incredible toys were only created to be enjoyed. I sincerely hope that everyone reading this book can employ these principles to attract every toy that I've had the good fortune to play with. And then some. I'm not asking that you don't hold these toys. I'll say it again, I'm just asking that you *hold on* to them. That you don't become attached to them.

EMBRACING EVOLUTION

And let me add that while redefining what *rich* means to you might be the most obvious change I ask you to make, the concept of transformation will be a thread that runs throughout and connects every principle in this book.

Though we are all capable of evolving, very few of us have faith in our ability to do so. We begrudgingly accept the inevitability of change when it comes to our physical form, but often fight it tooth and nail when it comes to our emotional and spiritual state. The yogis, however, know that fighting change is a losing battle, because God is going to change every single one of us, whether we like it or not. As Lord Buddha told his disciples, "Freedom and happiness are found in the flexibility and ease with which we move through change."

One of the principal goals of this book is to help you find a way to break free from a lifestyle that's holding you down and then find the courage to embrace one that uplifts you. To transform from someone who moves unconsciously through the world to someone who becomes the Super Rich individual I spoke of earlier, the individual who's completely aware of and completely at ease with everything around him. No matter where you're from or what you've done, you're never stuck in a particular circumstance, relationship, or cycle unless you say you are. Instead, you should take great comfort in the knowledge that each sunrise presents another day to do things right. If it feels like your life has become a nasty, brackish puddle of water, never forget that you do possess the power to transform it into a beautiful, rushing stream that will carry you to enlightenment.

My yoga teacher, Lady Ruth, has a very succinct, yet incredibly profound, way of articulating this truth. She teaches that you must approach life like riding the subway. When you realize that you're going the wrong way, you don't stay in your seat. Instead, you get up, get off your train, go to the opposite track, and get on one heading the other way. Your approach to life shouldn't be any different.

From time to time, we all find ourselves going the wrong

way in life. Just by picking up a book like this, you're acknowledging that you need to switch trains. Hopefully the principles
you're about to learn will provide you with the motivation and
inspiration to start going the other way.

THE SOURCES

Finally, before we go any further, I need to make the same dis-
claimer that I shared at the beginning of *Do You!*: Nothing in
the book should strike you as new. I'm not suggesting that I've
"discovered" or "created" any of these principles. Instead, I
freely admit to having learned them from the countless sources
and individuals that have inspired me over the years. This book
is nothing more than a wake-up call, a buzzing in your ear to
snap you out of the stupor you've fallen into and remind you to
embrace the truths you already know.

As you read, you'll notice that the vast majority of the principles I discuss, or wise men I quote, are either influenced by
or directly connected to the teachings of yoga. In particular,
I've been deeply inspired by two of the ancient holy scriptures
I mentioned earlier, the Yoga Sutras and the Bhagavad Gita. If
you're not already familiar with them, the Sutras are nothing
less than a textbook for the science of happiness and success,
while the Bhagavad Gita, or "Song of God," is perhaps the most
beloved book in the Hindu tradition.

I realize that many people reading this book, especially
those steeped in the Judeo-Christian tradition, might feel like
they're treading on new ground. But while my words might
often be articulated through the language of yoga, they're not
promoting anything different from what's found in the Bible,
the Koran, the Torah, or any other of the great spiritual books.

These books all promote the same truths and push us toward the same goal: enlightenment.

There are some yogis who teach that once you reach a state of complete enlightenment, or *Samadhi*, then you will turn into a fiery ball of light.

Suffice it to say, I don't expect to hear about anyone bursting into flames after reading this book. Principles like needing nothing, total acceptance, and *Ahimsa* (being non-harming in your relationship with the world) are extremely difficult to follow on a daily basis. So please don't become discouraged if you feel like you're falling short of them at first. Again, accept that by picking up this book, you're already moving toward a better space.

I'm certainly no saint and I'm not asking anyone else to be one either. (As you'll see, the only saint that I'm on intimate terms with is St. Bart's.) All I ask you to understand is that no matter who you are or what your circumstances are, you have faith that you can take control of your consciousness. It will take courage and consistent practice, but when you do that, you will be able to transform your relationship with yourself and the world for the better. You will be Super Rich.

ATTRACTING
THE WORLD

All nature loves an honest person. He need not run after things; they will run after him.
—Sri Swami Satchidananda

Every one of us has a unique gift that they'd like to share with the world. Maybe it's a novel written in our spare time, an idea for a new Web site or a concept for a children's clothing line. The question we often grapple with is how to get that gift out of our heart and into the world where it can be loved and appreciated?

When it seems like everyone is hustling and trying to "make it," how can you ensure that you're the writer who finds a buyer for his screenplay? The entrepreneur who finds an investor for his Web site? The designer who convinces a major chain to pick up her clothes? How can you ensure that you're the person who, rather than fruitlessly chasing success, actually has the world "run after" you?

The answer lies in two simple steps. The first is making sure that your gift is an honest expression of what's in your heart. In other words, you write the screenplay that's burning a hole through your brain, not the one you think might be the easiest to sell. You design the Web site that speaks to your passion, even if you think you'll have a hard time getting investors. You design the babies' clothing line that you think kids will look the cutest in, not the one that looks like every other line you see in the stores.

The second step is that rather than keeping that gift locked in your heart until you "find the right deal" or get someone to "pay me what I'm worth," you simply hand it over to the world. Without a contract. Without a deal in place. Without anyone even paying you a dime.

I realize that, as Rev Run cautioned me, a person struggling to pay off his electricity bill might not be too receptive to the idea that the quickest route to *get* what he needs is actually to start *giving* away his gifts. It probably sounds counterintuitive at best, downright foolish at worst.

Indeed, after I recently Tweeted the message, "to be a great getter, you have to be a greater giver," someone going by @Walltariq replied: "@UncleRUSH I understand your messages, but they only work for the folks that don't have the stresses of the middle class." So, for Tariq, and anyone else who might question how giving away his gifts will solve his day-to-day problems, I'd like to share some examples from the world of hip-hop that prove how giving can be the quickest and most honest way to attract the world's attention.

GIVE IT
(UNTIL THEY CAN'T LIVE WITHOUT IT)

One of the biggest misconceptions about the music industry is that the best way to get a deal is to approach a record executive out on the street outside his label, spit a hot verse or sing a beautiful hook for him on the spot, and then get invited upstairs to sign on the dotted line.

In fact, the best way to get a deal is to forget about the labels and instead just start giving away your music for free. Post it on the Internet. Share it on Facebook. Hand out free CDs. Never pass up any opportunity to share your gift with the world. From Lil Wayne to Drake to my nephew Diggy, I've watched many rappers use this method to take their careers to incredible heights.

When you can give honestly from what's inside you, the labels are going to come looking for you. They're going to want to find the person who's generating much love and enthusiasm. And when they find you, they're going to reward you very handsomely. Certainly more handsomely than if you had come to them begging for a deal.

Following this principle is certainly how I was able to jump-start my own career. Back in 1978, I was a little-known party promoter when I hooked up with Robert "Rocky" Ford and J. B. Moore, two workers at *Billboard* who were looking to establish themselves as record producers. After hooking up with a young rapper from Harlem named Kurtis Blow, they sank two thousand dollars—which represented all their savings—into recording and then pressing a single with him called "Christmas Rappin'."

Rocky and J. B. weren't sure how to create a buzz for Kurtis, so after learning about my connection to hip-hop as a party promoter, they enlisted me to help spread the word. It was a job I was happy to take on, because after listening to "Christmas Rappin'" I knew it had the potential to be a major hit.

Now if Kurtis had been a rock 'n' roller or a soul singer, I would have simply taken the record to the various labels in Manhattan and tried to shop for a deal. But since Kurtis was a rapper, I knew that route would only lead to a dead end. Back then the labels thought hip-hop was nothing more than a novelty, a fad whose days were numbered. If somehow I had managed to get a meeting with those executives, they would have kicked me out of their office the moment I started playing a rap record for them.

So instead of wasting my time with the labels, I started giving away copies of "Christmas Rappin'" to whomever I thought might play it. I gave it to the DJs at Leviticus, Bentley's, and Constellations, the popular R & B clubs in Manhattan. Then I gave it to the DJs at hip-hop clubs like the Disco Fever and Club 371 in the Bronx and The Rooftop and Small's Paradise in Harlem. Then I gave it to the DJs at gay clubs like Paradise Garage and The Loft, which were particularly influential with radio DJs. Then I went to WBLS and gave a copy to Frankie Crocker, who at the time was the hottest radio personality in the city. I gave away copies of that record to everybody and anybody I could think of until I didn't have anymore left.

And the strategy worked. A few DJs started playing it, and after the crowd went nuts every time it came on, word spread that "Christmas Rappin'" was a hot record. Then, realizing a buzz was building, we came up with a little "trick": We pressed up new versions of the record with an order number from Polygram Records on it. As the song started getting even more and more spins, the record stores started calling up Polygram asking to order a copy of "Christmas Rappin'." Obviously Polygram had no idea what the stores were talking about, but seeing that there was a heavy demand for the record, they managed to track us down and sign Kurtis to a deal (the first for a rapper with a major label). With Polygram's support, soon we had a bona fide hit and "Christmas Rappin'" would go on to sell more than five hundred thousand copies (I believe that it was only the second twelve-inch single, after Barbra Streisand and Donna Summer's "No More Tears," to go gold). It established Kurtis as a rap superstar and yours truly as a legitimate player in the game.

Of course, if we had insisted on getting a deal for the record *first*, we might still be waiting today. If we hadn't given away the record, the DJs wouldn't have heard it, let alone play it. And if the DJs hadn't played it in the influential clubs, the stores wouldn't have ordered it. And if the stores hadn't ordered it, Polygram would have never given Kurtis a deal. Eventually we would have had to go to the labels with our hats in hand and without the benefit of the leverage all the buzz had created. The labels would have undoubtedly kept rejecting the record until we became frustrated and eventually gave up on our dreams. Giving from the beginning, however, is what turned those dreams into a reality.

My experience with "Christmas Rappin'" showed me the possibility for attracting the world through giving, but perhaps the greatest contemporary example of this principle in practice is that of 50 Cent.

Certainly any conversation about the most successful artists in hip-hop, or all of pop music for that matter, would have to include 50 Cent. Yet even though 50 might be a superstar today, he hasn't always held that position. In fact, he was actually stuck on the sidelines of the rap game for many years until he was able to harness the power of attraction by giving away his music.

50's first foray into the business came in 1996, when as a twenty-one-year-old he signed a deal with my late, great friend Jam Master Jay of Run DMC, who had started his own label. 50 recorded an entire album with Jay, but it was never released and the two eventually parted ways. Despite that setback, 50 kept playing his music for whomever would listen to it until he finally caught the attention of The Trackmasters, a well-respected production duo who signed him to a deal with Columbia Records. Under their tutelage things started looking up, and 50 soon released a hit single called, "How to Rob." But before he could build on that success, he was infamously shot nine times in his Queens neighborhood. Then, to literally add insult to injury, Columbia decided to drop him while he recuperated from his wounds.

Finding himself without a deal and quickly losing whatever momentum "How to Rob" had generated, 50 decided to take an innovative approach to reviving his career. Most artists in his position would have started looking for another label deal, especially since they'd already made it over the hump twice. Without a deal, how would they eat? Or, even more importantly to some, how would they be able to maintain the "trappings" of a rapper who'd already had a hit?

But 50 didn't get ensnared in that anxiety. Instead, he simply started giving his music away for "free" via mix-tapes and the Internet. 50 figured that by giving away as much of his music as possible, he could corner the street market and, in doing so, once again attract the labels' attention. Whatever he might initially lose in earnings, he would more than recoup through creating legions of loyal fans. Fans who would actually be first in line to buy his "real" albums once he was able to get a deal.

50 had courage because he knew all he had to focus on was making music honest enough to inspire both him and the streets. He might have been a kid from Queens, but he instinctively understood Sri Satchidananda's quote at the top of this chapter: When you're honest, the world is going to run after you.

And 50's music was particularly raw and candid, even by hip-hop standards. He rapped about growing up hustlin' drugs, about his mother's murder, and of course about being shot all those times. 50's reality might have been off-putting to some and even downright disturbing to others, but it was his truth. And he never shied away from sharing it through his music.

The streets, true to the Swami's word, ended up falling head over heels in love with 50's music. They clamored for his mixtapes and downloaded his songs off the Internet. The buzz around him eventually became so loud that it made its way to the ears of Eminem, who signed 50 to a million-dollar record deal.

The rest, as they say, is history. But that transformation from an artist on the fringe of the industry to one of its biggest stars was only possible because 50 was willing to give his gift to the world *first*. Like any good spiritual warrior, he shared without any expectation for immediate compensation. And of course, by doing so, he ended up with more money than he probably imagined in his wildest dreams (and I bet 50's dreams are pretty wild).

I realize I've been talking a lot about hip-hop so far, but I want to stress that this principle applies to every profession and every walk of life. This is how careers are built in every industry. You give until they can't live without it.

So if you're a clothing designer who's looking to break into the fashion industry, just start making the designs that you feel in your heart and you think will make other people happy. (You also better move to New York City and start hanging out on Seventh Avenue, where the design companies are. Because you're never going to make it happen living in Cleveland or Chattanooga.) Just keep being sweet and honest, not only in your designs, but in how you interact with the people around you. If you meet another designer who needs help getting her show together, lend her a hand, without worrying whether you're going to get paid or credited for your work. Stay focused on giving, both in terms of your own designs and your relationships with others in the industry. Trust me, word will begin to spread around Seventh Avenue that you're a talented designer as well as a generous, confident, and happy person. By the time you've gotten your own line together, you'll look to your left and the funding you need will be there. Then you'll look to your right and you'll find the distribution you've been waiting on. Then you'll look at your feet and the media coverage that will introduce your line to the world will be lying there as well. Everything you need to be a success will be within your reach because you've become a magnet that pulls the world toward you.

That magnet, however, will only be effective if it's constructed out of a combination of focus, hard work, and sweet spirit. If you aren't excited to dedicate countless hours composing your music, or spend your weekends working on your designs while everyone else is out partying, then your appeal might not be as strong as it needs to be. Or if you put in the work, but with a mean, selfish energy, then your pull won't bring in everything that it is capable of either. I can only promise you that this principle will work if you're truly committed to focus, hard work, and generosity.

GIVING
UNCONDITIONALLY

I'm always struck by how many people fail to see the connection between giving and attraction. People will tell me they're writers but aren't writing anything at the moment because it's hard to find writing gigs these days. Or they're great chefs but aren't working at the moment because they're self-trained and right now restaurants are "only hiring people who've graduated from culinary school."

Whenever I hear that sort of talk, I say, "Stop making excuses and go do what you're supposed to be doing! And you can start by cooking me a nice vegan meal if you've got too much time on your hands!" Imagine if a comedian said, "Sorry, but I can't be funny right now because no one's paying me." Man, it's a comedian's job to be funny *all* of the time. Whether it's in the barbershop, at an open mic night, or on his own HBO special. Whether he's getting paid or not, he can never stop making people laugh. The moment he stops giving away his humor, he stops being a comedian.

And it's the same for writers, chefs, lawyers, doctors, or whoever. If you ain't giving away your gift, then you ain't in the game. And if you ain't in the game, then you're never going to win.

This is why you must release any concern that when you hand off your gift you won't receive anything back in return. As the yogis say, "You never lose what you have given." In that spirit, try to think of life as similar to running a relay race in which God is your teammate. You have to have faith that if you train properly and then run as fast as you can once the race starts, when the moment comes for you to hand off your baton (or your gift), God is not going to drop it. You have to believe that God is going to take that baton and run like the wind until it reaches the finish line.

When you give freely of yourself, you're going to be able to attract a divine teammate. A teammate who's going to take your mix-tape and run with it until you're a platinum-selling artist. A teammate who's going to take your recipes and passion for food and run with them until you're the chef of your own restaurant. A teammate who's going to take every honest and helpful idea that you have and run with it until it flowers into all its beauty for the world to see.

NEVER NEEDY

While giving is the most crucial component in attracting the world, another important skill is learning how to move through life without being, or at least appearing, needy. This is because when you chase things, they will always run from you. It's true in nature, in business, in relationships, and in every situation you might find yourself.

Picture a little girl trying to feed a peanut to a squirrel. Even though her mother warns her not to get too close, the girl desires a connection with the squirrel, so she runs to it. But of course the squirrel becomes frightened and scampers up the closest tree. The girl could chase the squirrel all day, but she'd never catch it.

The girl's only chance is to sit down on the grass and quietly hold the peanut out in front of her. If she doesn't move for several minutes, while radiating all the peace, love, and honest intention that is in her heart, the squirrel will be put at ease and eventually come over and take the peanut right out of her hand.

If you want to get paid and be a success at whatever you do, you must channel the sweetness and peacefulness of that little girl and carry it with you through life. When you can do that, then the world will be eating out of your hand just like that squirrel! You'll be able to get whatever toys you want without lifting a finger!

The opposite, however, is true as well: If you go running after money and success, they're just going to scamper away from you. As a boss, I can tell you if I look into the eyes of a potential business partner and all I see are dollar signs, I'm going to metaphorically run away. I'll be pleasant and cordial, but I've already mentally written you off. I simply don't feel comfortable doing business with people who chase things, especially money. No matter what the scenario, neediness is always a turnoff.

MONEY IS INSECURE

Given the unlimited power of attraction, it's very important that your gift emanate from the kind of sweet and honest spirit that I just mentioned. This is because if your gift arises from a negative or dishonest space, the energy you attract from the world will be very damaging. A classic example of this phenomenon is the pimp.

As everyone in the streets can tell you, the pimp-ho dynamic is built on the illusion that the pimp won't chase his ho (I say "his," but there are plenty of female pimps too). That's because pimps understand all too well that not chasing something is actually the quickest way to get it.

Even more than the threat of violence or the lure of money, this illusion of indifference is the pimp's most powerful tool in convincing insecure women to work for him. The pimp will lie and act like he doesn't love his ho, that he could walk away from her without a second thought. As a result, the ho is perversely attracted to the pimp. She'll follow him to infinity in a fruitless attempt to win his approval and make him "care."

Yet while the pimp might start off with flashy cars and fancy rings, whatever success he experiences will always be fleeting. The evidence can be seen on the streets, which are littered with broken-down, penniless, drug-addicted former pimps. And those are the lucky ones—most pimps end up in the morgue with a needle in their arm or a knife in their back.

What pimps always fail to understand is that when your magnetism is rooted in exploitation rather than service, in violence rather than peace, and cold-heartedness rather than compassion, the energy you attract will be so toxic that it will rot you away from the inside before you get a chance to enjoy any of the toys.

Essentially, since the pimp gives the world a damaged, dirty spirit, that's all he'll ever attract: damaged dirt. While the pimp can always pull a ho with his magnetism, he can never pull a nun. The nun is too in touch with her own compassionate and honest spirit to react to a spirit as negative and deceitful as that of the pimp.

We want to emulate the pimp's power of attraction, but rather than attracting the world with lies and greedy manipulation, we want to focus on attracting it through honesty and a lack of expectation. We want to be so pure in our spirit and intentions that when we give the world our gift, we don't spend a moment worrying about when we're going to receive a response, let alone a payment, for it.

Of course reaching such a state is a process. A process that this book will hopefully accelerate for you, but one that will still require hard work, dedication, and faith. That's why if you find it difficult to be completely honest and selfless, then it's OK to fake it just a little bit for the time being. In yoga, we're always told to smile whenever we encounter a difficult pose. We might feel like grimacing, or even crying, but as long as we keep smiling despite our difficulties, one day we'll get down in that pose and find that the smile is actually genuine. The smile, even when it feels forced at first, is what gives us the strength to continue the process.

The process of giving without expectation is no different. Even if you can't fully embrace this concept at first, if you can at least walk around with a smile on your face and make other people happy, you're going to get paid. At the VERY least.

This is because, like a ho, money itself is insecure. Never forget that money is more like the ho and happiness is like the nun. To get pure happiness, you're going to have to really give of your self. But with money, you can fake it a bit. Even if you just show the world a fraction of the sweetness and honesty that's in your heart, it's going to come running after you.

I know there are some of you who will say, "Make a million dollars from just sharing a fraction of my sweetness and honesty with the world? I'm good with that!" But trust me, while you might be good with that, you're better than that too. And this is a point I'm going to drive home throughout the book.

DON'T CHASE THE MONEY

Even though I'm going to keep encouraging you to look past the money, I want to make it clear again that when I ask you to focus on looking inside for your strength and happiness first, I actually view that as very concrete financial advice.

Certainly any success I have experienced as a businessman is due in large part to the fact that I've poured my passion into ventures that made me happy—even joyous—before they ever made me a red cent. Whether it was in the music, clothing, film, or even financial services industries, I've only chased things that I thought would make others happy. Never money.

That's been true since the start of my career, when Rick Rubin and I were running Def Jam Records out of his dorm room at New York University. Even though we were so desperate for funding that we literally begged a bank for a loan (as famously re-created in the movie *Krush Groove*), making money was never our primary concern. I can honestly say that when we showed up for work each morning (to say nothing of the countless nights we slept at the office), what motivated us wasn't the money, but the fun and happiness we experienced helping make hip-hop records and then sharing them with the world.

It might seem hard to believe in an era where rappers like Jay-Z and 50 Cent routinely make *Forbes*'s list of the richest entertainers, but back in the early eighties it didn't seem like there was *any* money in hip-hop even if we had been chasing it. At that time the labels were only looking for records similar to chart toppers like Prince's "When Doves Cry," or Lionel Richie's "All Night Long." These were the types of records the labels thought would sell and, as a result, were the only types of records they wanted to invest their money in.

So although I respect Prince and Lionel tremendously as artists, I have no doubt that if Rick and I had focused on records that sounded like them in order to have had a better chance at making money, we wouldn't have attracted very much success.

Our hearts wouldn't have been in producing that sort of

music and as a result we probably would have never made it out of Rick's dorm room, let alone become a top label in our own right. But by committing ourselves to uncompromising hip-hop tracks like T La Rock's "It's Yours," Run DMC's "Sucker MC's " or LL Cool J's "I Need a Beat," which made us happy, we were able to harness the energy and passion required to overcome the industry's perception that hip-hop was just a flash in the pan.

In fact, if you were to ask me to name my happiest moment from those early days (or at least the ones I can remember), I would say it was listening to the final mix of "Sucker MC's," while lying on the floor of the Greene Street recording studio in Manhattan. Hearing that drum clap kick in, I kept saying over and over, "Wait till these niggas hear this! Wait till they hear this!" I must have said this one hundred times! "Sucker MC's" was such a loud, aggressive, rebellious record—it felt like we were making ghetto punk rock. It was one hundred percent the opposite of a track like "When Doves Cry." In fact, I had zero expectations for how the world was going to react to that song. I didn't think it would get any airplay. But I knew for sure that it was going to blow hip-hop heads off! And the thought of that made me ecstatic!

I can't make the same claim, however, about getting a huge check after selling Def Jam many years later. Don't get me wrong, I'm sure it was reassuring to know that I wouldn't have to worry about money for a long time. But the truth is I honestly can't remember how I felt or where I was when I got that check. That's because holding that check in my hands wasn't magical. You might not believe me, but I'm keeping it one hundred!

The moments when I heard "Sucker MC's" or Public Enemy's "Rebel Without a Pause" for the first time are what I'll cherish till the end of my life. The happiness I received, and continue to receive, from those records is what makes me rich. Not the money I made from selling them.

I'm certainly not the first, or the last, person who's made a million dollars by chasing what made him happy. In fact, I know that the vast majority of millionaires have followed a similar path. Though I've never spoken to him specifically about it, I doubt my friend Paul Allen helped found Microsoft because he thought it would help him buy a four-hundred-foot yacht. Instead, Paul and his buddy Bill Gates were computer geeks who loved to sit around tinkering with operating systems. So when they realized they could develop one that might change the way people used computers, they probably thought it was the coolest thing in the world. Just as I couldn't stop thinking, "Wait till these niggas hear this," while listening to "Sucker MC's," Paul and Bill were probably thinking, "Wait till the other geeks see this," when they first came up with their original operating system.

When we picture a Microsoft or a Def Jam today, the first thing some people see is a dollar sign. But I promise you that the successes of those companies were rooted in a conscious pursuit of happiness, not in a blind pursuit of money.

You might "be good" with making money, but you're actually promised so much more than just that. That's why you want to try to use the principles in this book to learn how to give ALL of your heart, ALL of your sweetness, and ALL of the honesty that's in your heart, and you're going to experience a richness that supersedes any sort of material wealth. You're going to experience what it's like to be Super Rich.

SUCCEEDING

THROUGH STILLNESS

To the mind that is still, the whole universe surrenders.
—LAO-TSU

Most people sleepwalk through their lives. They fall in and out of love, hold down jobs, raise families, worry about the past, and dream about the future, but for all that activity, they are never truly awake. Despite the tremendous energy they exert trying to "get ahead," they never actually engage more than a very small part of their brain. The rest of their mind lies dormant, waiting for a wake-up call that often never comes.

The primary reason they remain in this state of unconsciousness is because they've become separated from stillness. Every single one of us is born with an endless supply of peace and tranquility in our hearts. Yet many of us lose sight of that stillness. We become so distracted by the noise of the world that we forget how much love and inspiration we already have inside of us, just waiting to be brought out into the world.

When Albert Einstein developed the theory of relativity, he was operating out of a state of stillness. When Biggie Smalls wrote his greatest rhymes, he was operating out of a state of stillness. When Thomas Edison invented the lightbulb, he was operating out of a state of stillness. When Gandhi went on his first hunger strike, he was operating out of a state of stillness too.

Stillness is the fertile soil in which imagination is nourished, and ideas can grow to incredible heights. The stillness inside of us is a field of dreams from which we can reap our most abundant harvests.

The great thinkers share an ability to access that stillness naturally. They can shut out the distractions and become totally connected with the inspiration and imagination that's inside them. They seem to know where the dial is that can turn down the noise and turn up their focus.

The rest of us, unfortunately, aren't wired that way. While we have great ideas, because we're disconnected from that stillness, those ideas are rarely given a chance to grow. Our hearts are screaming out instructions, but we can rarely hear them.

That's why in this chapter I want to introduce you to (or, if you're already familiar, refocus you on) the practice of meditation, which can help the noise of the mind subside to a point where you can achieve a state of what I call "super consciousness." A state in which rather than only operate off a fraction of your brain's capacity, you can unlock your mind and begin firing on all your mental cylinders.

CLEARING
OUT THE CLUTTER

Before I go any further, let me clarify what exactly I mean by "stillness." We all know the literal definition of the word, which is the lack of movement. But when I refer to "stillness," I'm actually referring to a quiet, peaceful mental state that allows you to be completely present in life. A state of what I call "pure presence," in which you're more connected to the world and as a result you experience moments that feel sharper and more intense than your normal existence.

Maybe you've already experienced some of the more extreme examples of pure presence. When you went bungee jumping and it felt like it took forever to hit the ground, you were experiencing pure presence. When you got mugged and while you were handing over your wallet it felt like everything was moving sloooooooow, you were experiencing pure presence. When you were in a car accident and it seemed like an eternity between the time you first jammed on the brakes and you actually hit the other car, you were experiencing pure presence.

Moments of pure presence can also be quite mundane. For example, the instance you "get" a funny joke, you're experiencing a moment of presence. When the movie you're watching becomes so intense that you stop breathing, you're experiencing a moment of presence. When you hear the melody of your favorite song and instinctively start singing along, that's a moment of presence as well. All those moments are shocking you into presence.

Those are the moments when you are at your happiest and most connected. But those moments don't occur as often as they could. While the world is filled with funny jokes and beautiful melodies, we miss the vast majority of them. We allow the distractions to steal our attention away from the miracles that are constantly unfolding around us.

To put it another way, try to think of your mind as an e-mail in-box and the distractions of the world as junk mail. If you don't clear out that junk mail, you're not going to be able to receive all the valuable messages of inspiration, beauty, and love that the world's trying to send you. You'll receive the bungee jump or the car crash, as well as the occasional joke and sunset, but you'll still only be receiving a fraction of what you're capable of receiving. One of the reasons meditation is such a powerful tool is because it helps you delete that junk mail and makes space for the inspirational messages you want to be getting.

Meditation certainly isn't the only tool that can help you clean out the clutter and noise. Some people can do it by jogging, listening to music, praying, or being completely engrossed in their work. But the practice that's proven the most effective at promoting stillness for me has definitely been meditation.

For instance, there's no doubt that meditating has helped me become a much more effective leader. In the past, I was an extremely difficult person to work both for and with. I've always brought a lot of passion and energy to the job, but it wasn't always focused. An employee might ask me to sign off on a project or try to explain a situation to me, but because I wasn't listening closely, I might make the wrong decision, or give them the wrong answer. Or worse, I'd blow up at them, not because they'd done anything wrong, but because I was frustrated by not having a complete grasp of what was going on around me.

Now that I meditate, even though I still slip up from time to time, I am much more connected to what people are telling me. As a result I can make more informed decisions on the issues that come across my desk. I'm also much less likely to lose control of my emotions and my words. It used to be if someone said something that rubbed me the wrong way, or simply wasn't what I was trying to hear, I would pounce on them. The music industry in particular is filled with people who can tell you how I would fly off the handle at what I perceived to be even the slightest offense or provocation.

These days, those kinds of frustrating moments seem to just roll off my back. It's not that I'm any less passionate, or have become less willing to fight for what I believe in. Instead, meditation has made me realize the futility of getting worked up about things I can't control—which is essentially everything.

One of the things I love about meditation is that you can go into a session ticked off about a pointless conference call you just sat through, or fed up with your girlfriend, and after a few minutes of sitting in silence, those problems won't even be on your radar anymore. We've all heard the saying, "This too shall pass," but meditation provides us with proof that it's really passing!

Once you learn to let go of all the issues or problems that seem to be holding you down, you'll see that there's actually no limit to how successful you can be. Instead of being unsure about your direction, you will feel like you can see people making moves from a million miles away. When you're operating out of a calm, happy, focused, and more heightened space as opposed to a nervous and distracted one, you're going to be a beast at whatever you do.

If you're a rapper, when you operate out of stillness, you're going to murder every track that you get on. If you're a stockbroker, operating out of stillness will allow you to read the market like it's a children's book. If you're a teacher, operating out of stillness will make you the most effective and the most popular educator at your school.

And even though there are probably better uses for my resources than owning a professional basketball team, if I ever did I can tell you this: In addition to lifting weights and running, I would also make sure my players incorporated meditation into their training regimen.

That's because a basketball player with a calm mind is still going to feel in complete control when he rises up to take that big shot at the end of the game. The crowd might be screaming, his teammates and coach might be going crazy, but he won't hear a drop of that noise. As he rises up for the final shot, it will feel like the world is moving in slow motion. He might be thirty feet from the basket with defenders draped all over him, but that shot is going to feel like a layup. It's going to feel like throwing a stone in the ocean. Because when you're operating out of stillness, everything is easier.

STILLNESS SUSTAINED

One of the greatest benefits of meditation is that not only will it help you find success, but it will help you *sustain* that success as well. Most of the great ideas we have in life are born out of fleeting moments of stillness. That means that even if those moments lead to success, it's often very hard to find them again.

I experienced this firsthand after I helped create Def Jam Records. Though today I'm credited with being one of the visionaries behind the rise of hip-hop, my career was largely unplanned and instead was born out of my reaction to a moment of profound stillness I experienced while watching a rapper named Eddie Cheeba perform at a nightclub in Harlem. I had never heard anyone rap before, but watching him rhyme effortlessly over the beat, I felt unbelievably inspired. As the crowd went wild around me, I knew right then and there that hip-hop was my calling. I walked into that club sleeping on hip-hop, but that spark of stillness woke me the hell up! When I left, I was on a mission to act on that inspiration and become part of hip-hop one way or another.

Since I didn't have any talent for rapping myself, I began promoting hip-hop parties just so I could be around that energy on a regular basis. Promoting parties led to managing artists. And managing artists led to founding Def Jam. And whether it was through throwing parties, promoting artists, or putting out records, I was completely focused on and inspired by contributing to hip-hop culture.

But after over a decade at the label, I felt I had contributed all that I could. Def Jam had sold millions of albums, helped turn numerous rappers into superstars, and played a major role in introducing hip-hop to the masses, but I still found myself asking, "Now what?" That let me know it was time to move on.

It could have easily been a very frustrating, even depressing, stage in my life. After all my success at Def Jam, the world was waiting for me to duplicate it, to make another "hit." If I had to depend on another random moment of stillness striking before I came up with my next idea, it could have been a very long wait.

Thankfully, with the help of meditation, I haven't had to depend on random moments of stillness to inspire me. Instead, meditation has helped me learn how to look inside and then take the moments of stillness that I find and string them together. Having unlimited access to that stillness is how I've been able to stay both inspired and focused. Having access to that stillness is how I was able to come up with a *Def Poetry Jam* or a Rush Card or a Global Grind. Having access to that stillness is what has allowed me to keep thinking up new ways to give. It's what has allowed me to keep my career moving forward, instead of stalling after my initial success.

Not long ago I attended a conference with a guy who helped create a major social networking site. The site had become a huge brand, the kind that every Internet entrepreneur dreams of developing. Not surprisingly, everyone wanted to know what was the secret to his success; how had he come up with such a groundbreaking idea?

But from listening to his answers—just like I didn't have a clear plan for hip-hop before I heard Eddie Cheeba—I discovered he'd never had a clear idea for his site either. He'd probably just been very inspired by the Internet and the concept of social networking and kept dreaming and working until one day he looked up and realized he'd invented something great!

Now that he'd built a fantastic site, experienced a ton of success, and contributed everything he possibly could to his creation, he'd reached that "what's next?" stage of his career. And while the world will expect him to create another huge hit, if he can't find the same spark of inspiration that launched his career, he might not be so fortunate the next time around. He might not be able to find the path that will take him back to that creativity.

And I want to stress that this phenomenon doesn't just apply to people who have created multimillion-dollar corporations. Almost all of us are going to face a "what's next?" moment. If your life has been centered around raising a family, when your kids start to get a little older and aren't around as much, you might find yourself asking, "What's next?" If your whole career has been focused on getting off the sales floor and into management, once you get up into that office, it won't be long till you find yourself asking, "What's next?" If all your energies have been poured into building your dream house, once it's finally completed and you've hosted all the parties you can host, one day you're going to look at it and think, "What's next?" Meditation is going to help you find the answer very quickly.

I didn't get a chance to speak with that Internet CEO at the conference, but if I ever do bump into him again, this is what I'd tell him: Don't sit around hoping that another inspiration will walk up and smack you in the face the same way that first one did. Don't wait for another Eddie Cheeba moment.

Instead, I'd encourage him, just as I'm encouraging you, to jump-start that process with the help of meditation. To use meditation to bring him back to that stillness where all his good ideas reside. So that he'll never have to search for a new idea again, or wonder "what's next?" All his creativity and inspiration will be at his fingertips.

MY PATH TO MEDITATION

Even when I was just starting off in the music business and was living an incredibly fast-paced lifestyle, I was still looking for ways to slow things down so I could grab ahold of all the ideas and inspirations inside me. Too often, my thoughts felt like a monkey running wild in my head. I'd never considered meditation or yoga, but I instinctively knew that if I didn't find a way to calm that monkey down, then I was going to have a very difficult time harnessing my abilities and best ideas.

The first tool I employed to create a sense of stillness was steam. There was something about standing in a hot shower that relaxed me, that made me feel like I was starting to get that monkey under control. Whenever I had a lot going on in my life, or needed to sort out some issues, I'd take a long, hot shower and try to let the waves of my mind calm down a bit. Rick Rubin still likes to tell the story of how back when we were running Def Jam out of his dorm room, he came home one day to find it engulfed in a dense fog. When his eyes finally adjusted to the mist, he saw me sitting on a chair outside his bathroom, where I had turned on the shower and let it run on hot for over an hour. "My bad," I told him sheepishly. "I was stressed out on how to push that new LL Cool J single, so I figured some steam might help clear my head."

Luckily for Rick, as Def Jam started to blow up, rather than search for my inspiration in his shower, I was able to afford the real thing. My de facto office became the Russian & Turkish Baths in lower Manhattan, an old-school joint that was frequented by Hasidic Jews, Russian gangsters, and music industry veterans. I would spend as much time as possible in their 150-degree steam rooms, planning strategies with my partners, and even conducting meetings—with nothing but a towel on—with clients. As I explained to a newspaper reporter back then, "I like that I can get quiet down in here and think about what the next move should be."

But while the steam baths, both homemade and professional, certainly helped me slow down a bit, they still didn't allow the noise to subside to the point where I could be completely still. It would take the practice of meditation to do that.

THE EIGHT STEPS

My first controlled encounters with the stillness inside of me began after I started practicing yoga. There might not seem to be an obvious connection between what is perceived to be a physical pursuit like yoga and a mental one like meditation, but in fact they are both part of what are known as the "eight steps" of classical yoga. If you're not already familiar, the steps are:

Yama: Universal morality, consisting of truthfulness, nonviolence, abstention from stealing, nongreed, and nonharmful sex

Niyama: Personal observances such as cleanliness, contentment, hard work, dedication, faith, and focus, as well as study of scripture

Asana (or Seat): Body poses and the physical practice of yoga

Pranayama: Breathing exercises and the control of life force

Pratyahara: Control of the senses

Dharana: Concentration on one's purpose in life

Dhyana: Meditation and devotion on the Divine

Samadhi: Union with the Divine

Once you embrace any of these eight steps, it's only natural that you will want to explore the others as well. (For our purposes in this chapter I'm only going to focus on two of these—Asana and Dhyana—but my plan is to one day write a short book that focuses exclusively on these eight steps and their incredible value as a spiritual science of happiness.) As I mentioned, the first one that I embraced was Asana, or the physical practice. Once I began to take classes, I found myself drawn to the most obvious by-products of the physical practice: the increased flexibility and relaxation I felt after going through the poses, as well as getting to be around all the beautiful women that were in the class with me!

But the more comfortable I became on my yoga mat, the more I began to realize that the greatest by-products of my practice were in fact as much mental as physical. When I was able to become more conscious of practicing my asanas with the correct intentions, smiling and breathing evenly while moving calmly from pose to pose, I started to experience profound moments of stillness. Even though I was sweating like a slave in the middle of a crowded room, the world seemed to stand still in those moments. Even if it was only for a few seconds, I felt like I was able to glimpse *Samadhi*, or Union with God, which is the eighth and final step in yoga. Indeed, it is written in the Yoga Sutras, "Yoga means control of the fluctuations of your mind."

Once I was able to experience such an undiluted sense of stillness, the next logical step was for me to learn how to access it on a more consistent, and even deeper, level. Not to just be able to feel that way in class, but to learn how to master that stillness and carry it with me throughout my entire life.

It's a practice I've become deeply dedicated to. Every morning when I wake up, I roll over, light a candle, and try to spend at least twenty minutes in meditation. Sometimes I might end up going for forty minutes, but twenty is my minimum. There are mornings I feel extra tired or get up late, but I always try to fight through whatever obstacles I perceive are in my way and make the time for meditation.

I also don't limit myself to one session a day. If I feel like I need the noise to subside again, then I'll make time for another session after work. A friend who's a big player on Wall Street once noticed that I always seemed relaxed after work and asked me for tips on how to unwind. "It's simple," I told him. "Just meditate for twenty minutes." When he explained that it would be tough to find time to meditate because he needs to see clients after work or spend time with his family, I shared an old meditation adage with him: If you don't have *twenty minutes* to delve into your self through meditation, then that means you need *two hours*.

CALMING THE WAVES

Around the time I was finishing up *Do You!,* I took a trip to South Africa on behalf of the Diamond Empowerment Fund. The D.E.F. is an organization I helped create whose mission is to encourage the diamond industry to support higher education in African countries where diamonds are a natural resource.

One of the institutions the D.E.F. had partnered up with was The CIDA/Maharishi Institute, a free college in Johannesburg. The school's consciousness-based curriculum revolves around a style of meditation called TM, or Transcendental Meditation. Although I wasn't really that familiar with the specifics of TM at the time, I had heard wonderful things about the work the school was doing and looked forward to visiting during my trip.

When I arrived at the school I could see that those rave reviews were well earned. The students were obviously bright, alert, and energized with life, but they were also very still. They demonstrated a level of poise and control that seemed beyond their age and were certainly different from the students I had encountered in the countless schools, both private and public, that I've visited in the U.S.

During my visit I meditated and practiced yoga with the students, and then I gave a short speech in which I told them how thrilled I was to help support the school and how I hoped their example would encourage even more young people to move toward a conscious lifestyle.

After meeting with the students, I was asked to film a short interview for the school's Web site. As we prepared to tape, the interviewer asked me if I practiced TM myself. "Naw," I told him. "I meditate focusing on my breath, which is how I was taught in my yoga class. I know TM uses mantras, but for me just looking at my breath is enough to trick my mind into stillness." "I'm glad your style is working for you," the interviewer told me, "but I would still strongly encourage you to check out TM for yourself. I think you'll find it's more powerful than what you're used to." The guy was very polite and respectful, but from the way he spoke about TM, I could tell he wasn't playing. His passion piqued my interest, which had already been sparked by those impressive students. I decided that when I returned to New York I would check out TM for myself.

It's not that I was totally unaware of TM. I knew that the practice had been created by the legendary Indian guru Maharishi Mahesh Yogi and that during the 1960s it had attracted celebrities like the Beatles, the Rolling Stones, and the Beach Boys. (A trend that continues to this day: Jerry Seinfeld, Stevie Wonder, Howard Stern, and the director David Lynch all practice TM as well.) Yet despite TM's relatively high profile, I never really gave much thought to how it might differ from the kind of meditation I had already been practicing.

That changed after I returned to New York and linked up with a well-known TM teacher named Bob Roth (or, as I like to call him, "The Monk"). When I got Bob on the phone, I told him about my trip and asked if he could come over to my apartment and teach me the TM technique. "I'd love to," Bob told me. "But everyone has to pay a fee to learn TM. It's how we're able to fund schools like the one you visited. Normally the fee is about fifteen hundred dollars, though we provide scholarships to people who need some assistance. Given your financial situation, however, I'd suggest you make a donation for twenty-five hundred dollars."

When I heard that, my initial reaction was that Bob was trippin'. "Over two thousand dollars to learn how to meditate?" I said to myself. "When I've already been meditating every day for the last ten years? I'm not trying to pay that . . ." But the more I thought about it, it didn't seem quite as outlandish. It was true that I had been extremely impressed by what I saw in South Africa. So if I could write a check that would not only teach me how to improve my meditation, but potentially help thousands of children to do so as well, then that was money well spent. So I called Bob back and told him, "OK, I'm down. It sounds like fun."

When Bob and I finally sat down for my lesson, the first thing he did was explain the basic philosophy of TM. As he put it, the mind is like an ocean, with waves (your thoughts) on the surface and silence (the God in you) at its depths. Other styles of meditation teach that you need to calm those waves down before you can really "start" to meditate, which is why they promote "chasing" the thoughts out of your mind with your breath. TM, on the other hand, teaches that you don't have to force the issue. Instead the waves will eventually settle down on their own, allowing you to experience the transcendent— the field of silence within.

Bob also broke down how TM has a unique take on the use of mantras. In other forms of meditation, a mantra is usually a word or phrase that you repeat over and over again to help your mind become more still (for instance, in the past I had used the phrase "let go"). In TM, the mantras are only sounds or vibrations, without any connection to meanings or ideas. Also, in TM each student receives a personal mantra directly from their teacher, which has been specially suited for his or her age and personality.

And it's true, once Bob gave me my own mantra and I began repeating it in my head, the effect was astonishing. The waves subsided rather quickly and soon I was experiencing a depth of stillness that I hadn't reached before. When I finished meditating using the TM technique, the colors in my apartment seemed richer and my vision seemed sharper. I was hooked. After a few weeks of meditating using my mantra, I could see that the technique had increased the quality of my meditation significantly.

I've been practicing TM for more than three years now and it's been such a blessing. Bob actually lives down the street from me and has become a great friend. Whenever we're both in town at the same time, he'll come over in the morning and we'll do a meditation session together, such a beautiful addition to my day.

Bob's also the national director of the David Lynch Foundation, a nonprofit organization that has provided scholarships for more than one hundred thousand at-risk children to learn how to meditate using the TM technique. In addition to students, the organization also uses TM to help American Indians with high suicide rates, veterans from Iraq and Afghanistan who are suffering from post-traumatic stress disorder, and both prisoners and prison guards who have trouble dealing with the pressure cooker that is jailhouse life. The foundation is doing so many great things that I've recently joined its Board of Directors.

While I'm one hundred percent committed to helping the foundation spread the word about the value of meditation, I also understand there is a degree of skepticism about TM out there. To some, TM feels very rigid, especially when it comes to the use of mantras. It's true, TM people are very strict about their mantras and believe that if you don't get yours directly from a TM teacher then it's not "real." While I certainly respect how passionate TM people are about their technique, I tend not to get as wrapped up in the specifics as they do. To me, meditation is fun and anything that makes it too serious or stressful can be counterproductive.

SELF-MEDICATION
THROUGH MEDITATION

Any discussion on meditation wouldn't be complete without also acknowledging the impact the practice can have on your physical well-being. It might seem difficult to believe that simply sitting still for twenty minutes could make you healthier, but it absolutely does.

For instance, I've found that meditation gives me a real boost on mornings when I wake up with a headache or stuffed-up nose. In the past I might have gone back to bed or reached for some Advil, but now as long as I get up and put in those twenty minutes, I usually emerge from my session breathing great and with a clear head.

When I was in my twenties, I used to get sinus and throat infections all the time. I'm sure the cocaine wasn't helping matters, but outside of my lifestyle choices, I thought there was something seriously wrong with my body. When I went to see a few different doctors about it, they all told me that I had a deviated septum and that I'd never stop getting infections unless I had surgery. I seriously considered going under the knife, but after I started practicing yoga and meditating, the infections eventually went away. (It probably also helped that I stopped eating dairy and started using a neti pot, a device that washes out your sinuses with warm, salty water. It was created by yogis in ancient India, but now you can find them in any American drugstore.) The situation improved so much that prior to writing this chapter, I hadn't even thought about my sinus problems for many, many years. I literally went from preparing myself for surgery to forgetting that I even had a "problem."

Outside of my own experiences and observations, there's also plenty of irrefutable science attesting to the healing powers of meditation from groups like the National Institute of Health, the American Medical Association, and the American Heart Association. Additionally, studies from Harvard and Stanford have proven that TM develops the brain, increases creativity and intelligence, and reduces stress, anxiety, depression, and high blood pressure. (Some insurance companies even reimburse for TM instruction if you have high blood pressure.)

When I witness our national debate over health care, I wish people could realize how much physical suffering we could alleviate and money we could save just through promoting meditation. This is because at the very, very least, studies have proven meditation calms people's nervous systems (I know it's certainly calmed mine). And a calm nervous system helps build a much stronger immune system. From the common cold to cancer, your body will be much less likely to break down and get sick when you're operating out of the calm, steady state that meditation promotes. So if we could just improve the nervous systems of a few million Americans, we could heal so many without spending a dime.

Another area where meditation could not only alleviate

suffering but also save society a ton of money is in how we treat
people with substance abuse problems. As someone who has
gotten high a lot of times off a lot of different drugs, I know
what people are chasing when they smoke, drink, sniff, shoot
up, or pop pills. They're chasing that monkey I spoke of earlier.
They're using the drugs to drown out the noise in their heads
and help them feel just a little bit of stillness in their lives.

But here's the thing: The stillness you think you're experiencing on drugs is fake. It's nothing more than a Band-Aid, a
delusion that makes you believe the monkey is under control,
when in fact it's still running wild throughout your mind and
your nervous system. Because of their connections to mysticism,
some people tend to view meditation and drugs as different sides
of the same coin. I know from firsthand experience, however,
that they actually produce the exact opposite effect.

When you're high, your nervous system gets overworked
and your mind gets filled with noise.

Meditation, conversely, calms down the nervous system
and clears out all the noise. You can still hear the melodies and
laughter you hear when you're high, but without all the distractions. And when the distractions are gone, you can realize your
unlimited potential. You cannot only compose a beautiful melody, but you can also split an atom, invent a new technology,
perform a surgery, or write a poem. You can think a hole
through any idea that interests you. To put it most simply, the
mind on drugs is cluttered. The mind on meditation is clear.
And a clear, uncluttered mind is always the one that will take
you to your highest (no pun intended) heights.

That's why if you're struggling with drugs or drinking, I
really want to encourage you to give meditation a try. Trust
me, the substances are going to run you into the ground and

ruin you both physically and mentally. No matter how much you'd like to believe you're different, there's no escaping the destructive nature of drugs.

Meditation, conversely, is a sustainable practice. That means when you practice it, it not only helps you, but it helps the world around you too. Whereas drugs and drinking will not only destroy you, but also do serious damage to the people in your life (a sad fact that anyone who has loved an addict or substance abuser can attest to), meditation makes your connection to the people around you stronger and more loving.

The power of meditating over medicating was driven home to me not long ago when I was invited to speak about TM at The Doe Fund, a wonderful program in New York City that helps homeless men reenter society. A lot of guys in the program have dealt with very serious drug problems, so when I spoke at their facility in Harlem, I made sure to mention how meditation was a great alternative to the methods they had been using to deal with the noise in their heads and their sense of isolation.

The men listened with an openness that surprised and encouraged me. Before I spoke only a few had signed up to learn to meditate, but afterward the list filled several pages. So many have started and so many more are ready to start.

One of the men, named Richard, has posted an online testimonial to just how powerful an impact meditation has had on his life. He said that just a few weeks after starting to meditate, he'd already stopped getting high and had seen his life start to improve so much. In the video, Richard said that as long as he could remember, he instinctively knew the ancient truth of life, which is that we are all connected. "I have always known I am 'That,' you are 'That,' all of this is nothing but 'That.'" The problem, he said, was that he had never had confidence in that instinct and as a result went looking for peace and stillness in the wrong places. But when he started to meditate and go beyond the surface noise of his mind, he began to experience the connectivity he'd been searching for all those years out on the street.

It was a supremely enlightened realization. Students of the greatest yogis struggle for a lifetime to experience this sense of connectedness. And Richard found it in such a short time— not at the bottom of a bottle, or in a vial of crack, but in sitting in silence for twenty minutes every day.

MEDITATION AND YOUTH

Meditation over medication is particularly relevant when it comes to the lives of young people, as the teenage years are often when the noise in our heads is at its loudest. Too many young people try to muffle that noise by puffing on a blunt with their friends after school, or sneaking a few beers down in their parents' basement. I'm convinced, however, that if we can show teenagers that there's another avenue available to them when they begin to feel stressed out, insecure, depressed, or heartbroken, then they won't be so likely to head down the dead-end path of substance abuse.

Our youth need to know that through meditation they can find the peace and confidence they're seeking. They are our most precious natural resource and we must do all we can to give them tools that will help them stay focused and positive.

The other day I had a meeting with Chris Brown, the young R & B singer who unfortunately has become best known for the incident in which he hit his girlfriend, the singer Rihanna. Chris deserved all of the criticism he received for his actions, but I ultimately believe he deserves our forgiveness too. He's an intelligent and extremely talented young man who made a mistake. But he can, and I think he will, do better.

While we were talking, I mentioned my meditation practice and Chris immediately expressed interest in learning TM himself. I set him up with Bob and I have no doubt that as long as he sticks with it, he'll see that meditation keeps him grounded, at peace, and focused on his considerable gifts. I only wish that he had been exposed to meditation earlier in his life. If he had, I'm confident that the noise in his head wouldn't have gotten so loud that it drowned out his better instincts, that it caused him to make choices that created so much needless suffering in the lives of the people closest to him.

Chris is going to be fine, but there are countless other young people out there who are still at risk and desperately need the stability and peacefulness that meditation will bring into their lives. Studies have shown that young people exposed to meditation have higher test scores and better grades; consume less alcohol and drugs; and have fewer suspensions and expulsions, lower dropout rates, and higher graduation rates compared with non-meditating kids.

A few months ago I caught another glimpse of this firsthand when I visited the Ideal Academy in Washington, D.C., a school that has integrated meditation into its curriculum. The academy is in the middle of a very tough part of D.C. and, like a lot of hood schools, has seen its share of problems. But the school's principal, Dr. George "Doc" Rutherford, told me that once he introduced two fifteen-minute "Quiet Times" into the students' schedule, things began to improve dramatically.

After Quiet Time, teachers say their students are more alert and engaged. Parents say their kids are easier to get along with at home. And students say they feel less anger, less stressed, and better about going to school. Once one of the worst-performing schools in D.C., now the Ideal Academy has transformed, thanks to meditation, into one of the city's strongest.

And we're seeing this happen all around the country. Wherever kids are given a chance to be still, violence and absenteeism go down, grades go up, and both teachers and students report that the environment becomes much more conducive to learning. Yet despite the hundreds of success stories that are being reported around the country, there are some out there who want to stop schools from incorporating meditation into their curriculum. In the eyes of these shortsighted people, by encouraging young people to sit in silence and communicate with their higher selves, we will be undermining traditional spiritual values. Essentially, these people worry that by helping young people talk to the God inside of them, we'll be taking prayer out of the church and putting it directly into the hands of the people. And to them, that seems to be a scary idea.

I don't want to pass judgment on any Christian groups or any other group that feels threatened by meditation. Which is why I think schools should follow the example of the Ideal Academy, as it doesn't directly refer to meditation, but rather promotes Quiet Times. This gives the students the freedom to use the time however they choose—reading silently, meditating, praying, or just sitting still and not moving. Basically, I don't care what they call that block of time that's set aside for stillness, just so long as stillness is part of every student's day! If we really care about our children's future, we need to take meditation out of the margins and make it mainstream. Make it one of the basic tools we use in raising our children.

MEDITATION AND MY KIDS

While I can't control the curriculum in our nation's schools, I do have some say in what goes on with my own children. So you can be sure that I've started to introduce meditation into their lives.

I've noticed that when people look at pictures of my daughters online, they'll often make comments to the effect of, "Wow. They seem like such happy, grounded young ladies." And thankfully they are (though like all kids they have their moments). The vast majority of credit goes to their mother, Kimora, who's done such a wonderful job raising them. But I believe that meditation has also played a role in their demeanor. Both my daughters have started practicing TM with Bob and are already showing signs of being great meditators.

They both spend at least ten minutes in quiet time every day and by the time they're teenagers hopefully a regular twenty-minute session will be part of their daily routine. But more important than whatever number of minutes they spend in quiet time, I want them to understand that the peace and tranquility they feel after meditating is actually their natural state. That no matter what happens in the world around them, there's nothing that can disturb that pool of stillness that lies in their hearts.

And that's the message that I hope everyone reading this book can embrace. Realize that the sense of calm and peace you experience during those twenty minutes of meditation is not an aberration: That state of stillness is not a dream or "magic." Rather, it's your natural state, what you're capable of experiencing every minute of every day!

If you're still wondering whether meditation is something you need, ask yourself this: Where do you spend most of your time? In the stress and chaos of the world? Or resting in the perfection of your heart? If the honest answer is "the stress of the world," then you need to embrace the power of meditation. It's going to allow you to rest in perfection, which is where you always want to be.

FINDING YOUR INNER STILLNESS

• HOW TO MEDITATE •

Outside of its perceived rigidity, the main skepticism with TM seems to center around the fact that there is a charge for taking the course. As I said, I was skeptical about putting down my money at first as well. And even though I can say today that it was probably the best money I've ever spent, I also accept that fifteen hundred dollars is a tough check for most folks to write.

Seeing that you already paid your twenty-five dollars for this book, now I'd like to throw in for free some of those "expensive" tricks they teach in the TM course. If after reading this chapter you decide that TM might make sense for you, then maybe you'll go to TM.org and sign up for the class. But what I'm going to give you now is more than enough to get started. In fact, it could be all that you'll ever need.

Once you decide you're ready to try meditation, the first thing to do is find a quiet, comfortable place where you can sit relatively undisturbed for at least twenty minutes. I want to emphasize "relatively," because one of the most common problems novices experience is that they think they've become distracted by outside noises. When they hear their children playing in the next room, their neighbors walking around in the apartment above them, or a dog barking outside, they lose focus very quickly and give up before they ever really get going.

It's certainly nice if you can find a quiet space, but if you can't it shouldn't be a deal breaker. Personally, I've found some of my best sessions have come when there's been a lot of noise going on around me. My apartment overlooks the "Ground Zero" site in Lower Manhattan and every morning when I sit down to meditate, I can hear the cranes, bulldozers, tractors, and dump trucks doing their thing. Instead of letting those sounds distract me, I've found that they can actually be very inspiring, as they remind me to be present. The key is, rather than getting thrown off by the noise, try to embrace whatever you might hear when you sit down. As Eckhart Tolle writes, "Silence is helpful, but you don't need it to find stillness. Even where there is noise, you can be aware of the stillness under the noise, of the space under which the noise arises. That Is the inner space of pure awareness, of consciousness itself."

After sitting down and getting comfortable, the next step is to simply begin repeating your mantra. Since most of you reading this probably don't have one yet, let me share a mantra that I've been taught and have found works well for novices: Rum.

Try not to think of it as a word, but rather as a vibration. "Ruuuuuuuuuuum." Say it loudly in your mind. Say it softly. Say it fast. Say it slow. Whisper it. Scream it. Fixate your mind on "Rum" until that vibration fills up your being.

If you keep repeating "Rum" for even just five minutes, you'll feel yourself beginning to transcend the hundreds of frivolous thoughts that are cluttering your mind. Again, think of all those thoughts as waves on a stormy ocean. As the vibration of "Rum" becomes stronger and stronger, soon the fluctuations of those waves will become smaller and smaller until your mind will be a calm, glassy sea. When those waves are gone, you'll be entering a state of real stillness.

In addition to mantras, the technique that really separates TM from other schools is how it suggests you deal with distractions. Most of the yogic-based techniques teach that once you start meditation, it's imperative that you don't move physically, for fear that you will "break" your meditation. TM, however, teaches that if you're just starting to meditate and a fly lands on you, then it's OK to brush it off. Or if you have an itch, then scratch the hell out of it if that's what you want to do. The belief is that that itch will prove to be so distracting if you don't address it that you'll never be able to enter a state of stillness. By brushing or scratching that itch, you're allowing yourself to move forward with your meditation. And once you do reach that stillness, you'll be so happy that you won't care what's going on around you. Flies could be sitting on your arm, snakes could be crawling up your leg, birds could be landing on your head, and you wouldn't even blink, let alone brush them off. You wouldn't care. You'd be so content in your meditation that you'd have no interest in moving. When you're in deep meditation, even the sound of clearing your throat feels like you just set off a bomb. As you float on that glassy sea of stillness, you don't want to have anything to do with the physical world. The stillness feels so much sweeter.

TM promotes a similarly relaxed approach to dealing with the thoughts that might drift into your mind during meditation. While the goal is to stay focused on your mantra, it's OK if from time to time you lose sight of it. By that, I mean you might be able to focus on "Rum" for several minutes, but suddenly a thought will come into your head and you'll find yourself focusing on it instead. Rather than immediately trying to push that thought out of your mind, TM teaches that it's OK to engage it for a moment, to gently think it through if that's what you want to do. Eventually the vibration of your mantra is going to become more attractive to you than any thought.

I think this particular strategy is what's made the biggest difference for me. In the past, I was expending so much effort trying to breathe the thoughts out of my head that I was actually blocking my ability to be still. Now that I'm free to engage the thoughts and then let them go again, I've found that the thoughts actually come much less frequently, and when they do, I barely notice them.

Yesterday, for instance, I decided to meditate in my library around the same time my housekeeper was planning to clean it. A few minutes into my meditation, I could hear her knocking on the door to see if it was OK for her to come in. In the past, the knocking alone would have been a deal breaker, a distraction that would have completely disrupted my session. This time, however, I acknowledged it for a second and then let it go, because it seemed so unimportant compared to the stillness I was experiencing. As I meditated she even started cleaning up and vacuuming around me, but I still refused to come out of my stillness. I was enjoying the stillness too much to be bothered with the physical world, even something as potentially distracting as someone pushing a vacuum around my feet. In fact, despite all the noise around me, I actually had a particularly deep session.

MANTRA DEFEATS THE MONKEY

No matter what style of meditation you choose, the key to reaping its benefits is to be slow and steady, especially when you're new to the practice. As my good friend Deepak Chopra once told me when we were discussing meditation, the one thread that runs through every different style and technique is a slow, steady, and consistent approach. "There is no greater attribute in a meditator than patience," he said.

So while the first few minutes of your session might prove difficult, it is critical that you do not become discouraged and quit. No matter how much you focus on your breath or your mantra, that monkey still might break free in your head. It's tempting to start thinking, "Man, I'm never going to meditate. This isn't working." When you feel that way, just stay patient. If you keep going back to your mantra, suddenly you'll find yourself thinking, "Oh, shit! I am meditating!" And while that thought might get your mind running again, as long as you return to your mantra, eventually you'll slip back into the stillness. And the second time will be deeper than the first. You might get caught up in your thoughts three or four times, but as long as you keep going back to that mantra, eventually you'll slide in a little bit deeper each time, until finally you're all the way in, submerged in stillness.

The key is simply to not give up. Most people will quit in the first two or three minutes and never experience the stillness inside of you. Don't be one of those people. There's no need to beat yourself up if the stillness doesn't come easy at first. Do you look ripped the first time you do a set of push-ups? Of course not. Meditation is the same way. It might take a while before you start to "see" the results. Just make a commitment to those twenty minutes and have faith that it won't be long until you see those "mental muscles" starting to grow. Tell that monkey the same thing I tell him: "Nigga, I don't give a damn what you do or how much noise you make. Your ass is sittin' here with me for twenty minutes whether you like it or not! This body ain't moving!"

And if that grind starts to feel like too much and you catch yourself doubting your ability to meditate, then find some confidence in this basic truth: Your mantra will always defeat the monkey. The only way the monkey can win is if you give up and stop meditating. Otherwise, the vibration of your mantra is eventually going to chase him away for good. And when that happens, a profound and serene stillness is going to fill up that space.

Since I've already hit you off with a mantra, everyone reading this book is capable of achieving the state I'm promoting. You don't need another mantra, or a special room to meditate in. All you need is a little patience. We're just talking about a twenty-minute commitment here, folks. I'm not asking you to turn your entire day upside down, or take time off from work. Only twenty minutes of your time. No matter what excuse you might make, if you can sleep for eight hours, you've got twenty minutes for meditation. No matter who you are, or what your circumstances are, you always have twenty minutes to invest in yourself. Even if it feels like a grind at first.

THE WATCHER

When you make a real, lasting commitment to the practice of meditation, eventually you will be able to enter a state of "moving meditation." Despite its name, Moving Meditation doesn't refer to a physical state. Instead, it refers to a mental state where you are able to take all the calmness, contentment, and stillness you experience during meditation and transfer those feelings to the rest of your life.

This state will be the ultimate by-product of your meditation. As your commitment to meditation becomes more consistent, and your sessions last longer and go deeper, you will begin to experience little flashes of that same kind of stillness while moving through your day. Eventually, those flashes will last longer and come more frequently, until you've become what the yogis call "The Watcher."

The Watcher might sound like the name of a superhero (I think it actually was the alias of an old comic book character), but in fact anyone can be The Watcher in his day-to-day life. The doctor who comes up with the diagnosis that stumps all her peers is operating as The Watcher. The singer who hears a sweet melody in her head is operating as The Watcher. Just as that Internet entrepreneur who can always find the inspiration for new ideas is The Watcher too.

Those who are disconnected from stillness can only see what's right in front of them. It's as if they move through life with blinders on. But those who operate as The Watcher are able to see everything. It's like they have 360-degree vision.

So for instance, let's go back to that basketball player taking a potential game-winning shot. When a player who's disconnected goes up for that shot, all he's going to see are the defenders standing in his way, trying to prevent him from scoring. As a result, he'll be distracted and most likely miss.

But when a player who's The Watcher goes up for that shot, while he'll see those defenders, he'll be able to see the basket too. And because his mind will be so calm, like I said before, that basket will look as big as an ocean to him. There's no way The Watcher isn't knocking that shot down!

When you're The Watcher, you can see past the distractions and focus on whatever path you pursue. You're able to become a more effective basketball player, a more effective businessman, a more effective painter, a more effective philanthropist—whatever pursuit attracts your interest.

You'll be so in control of your thoughts, emotions, and actions that it will seem like you're not only directing, but also starring in the movie of your life. Instead of feeling like an extra waiting to be told what to do, you'll be the Steven Spielberg of your own existence. You'll be the one determining which scenes you like and which ones you want to do over. You'll be the one deciding when you want to stick to the script and when you want to improvise. And of course as the star of your own flick, you'll be the loving, happy, suave, upbeat character who outsmarts all the bad guys, finds the buried treasure, and gets the girl (or the guy) at the end!

Please believe me that if you can make this commitment to twenty minutes of meditation a day, your life will transform in ways you probably never dreamed possible. In fact, put this book down right now and go sit in silence for twenty minutes! Experience firsthand how beautiful and rewarding life can be when you're still!

THE WORK
THAT PRAYS

See the job. Do the job. Stay out of the misery.
—MAHARISHI MAHESH YOGI

While it's generally accepted that spiritual practices like yoga, meditation, and prayer can help speed up our evolution, too often we forget about another tool, one that we already employ every day, which is equally effective at accelerating our journey toward enlightenment:

Hard work.

On the surface, simply doing your job to the best of your ability might seem like it has very little to do with the practices I just mentioned. The truth, however, is that when you put your head down and work your hardest at any task, it's actually a very powerful form of moving prayer.

A teacher who is totally committed to educating the children in her classroom, a janitor who keeps his building looking immaculate, or a baker who makes perfect loaf after perfect loaf are all praying just as hard through their efforts as the yogi who spends his days chanting God's name.

Yet while almost everyone performs some sort of work each day, most people are not conscious of this connection between their work and their proximity to God. This is because they are too often preoccupied with the results of their work. Their focus is on how much money their work generates rather than the actual work itself. They fail to realize that when you view your work with both eyes only on the result, that work will never prove truly rewarding, either financially or spiritually. Never lose sight of the fact that the actual work that you do in life—the moment in which a teacher is engaged in drawing up a lesson plan, the janitor is mopping the floors, or the baker is rolling out dough—is the source from which true happiness will stem.

When you are able to stay focused on your work without any expectations for, or concern with, the fruit of your labor, there will be no limit to the heights you can reach. You will go from the dishwasher to the restaurant tycoon, from the assistant to the CEO. And not only will you be rewarded for your effort with money and recognition, but you'll also receive two much more valuable gifts: freedom and happiness.

As much as I cherish yoga and meditation, outside of spending time with my daughters, nothing makes me as happy, or feel as free, as sitting down at my desk each morning and becoming completely engaged in a piece of work. To take on a problem and become so focused on it and connected to it that it feels like time is standing still.

(A common misconception is that "times flies" when you're working your hardest. That when you're really plugged in, you'll look up at the clock and your shift will be over before you even know it. The truth is, however, when you're completely focused on a moment at work, time moves slowly. And that's how you'll want it to be. When you're totally tuned in, you won't even be thinking about when your shift is going to end.)

For some, heading to work is akin to heading to jail—they feel like they have to "serve" their time on the job. They're trying to escape their work rather than embrace it. I'm so thankful every day that I sit down behind my desk, I'm excited to be there.

I like to believe that I've been able to help my partners and employees develop a similar attitude toward their work. One of the greatest compliments anyone has ever paid me came when a magazine reporter asked my good friend and guru Shannon Gannon what it was like to work with me. "I wouldn't describe my relationship with Russell as 'work,'" replied Shannon, who, as one of the founders of Jivamukti Yoga, helped me create a yoga scholarship program for women of color. "I can't remember ever having 'worked' with Russell. Or imagine having to work with or for Russell. Of course he's serious about the things that matter to him in life, like his children, yoga, veganism, making money, etc., but he knows that the ultimate goal is enlightenment and that's about being happy and joyful."

God, it would be so beautiful if everyone I've "worked" with over the years felt the same as Shannon. There have been some, however, who only viewed our partnerships through the lens of how much money they either made or lost. But by doing so, I think they only served to cheapen their own experience. That's because if I've learned anything in twenty-five years in the entertainment business, it is that my only true rewards have been the work itself.

I'll say it again, no royalty check has ever made me happier than actually making a record like "Sucker MC's." I've never owned a car or even a house that's made me feel more joyous than I felt designing my first collection for Phat Farm. The labor alone is what has made me happy, never the fruits of that labor. Trust me, when you're consumed with seeing a material result from your work, you are going to miss out on the joy of *getting* rich.

PICKING UP THE TRASH

One thing that holds many people back from becoming great workers is a misguided belief that only certain jobs are worthy of their "A-game," or maximum effort. In this country, while we are quick to celebrate a Wall Street trader who works late hours every day, or a chef who spends countless hours perfecting his craft, we tend not to pay the same amount of respect to someone who shows a similar dedication to a "low-paying" or "low-profile" job. It's as if while we can see the wisdom in a chef being completely dedicated to his job, a dishwasher who demonstrates a similar work ethic is somehow foolish, or wasting his time.

Recently I was discussing this phenomenon with a friend when he cut me off and said, "Oh, then you really need to check out Taiwan. You'd be in heaven over there."

"Why's that?" I asked.

"Because most people take every job seriously in Taiwan," replied my friend. "I was just there visiting my wife's family and I couldn't believe how dedicated people were to their work. Conductors on the train, cashiers at the supermarket, bellhops at the hotel—everyone was grindin' their asses off. The craziest thing I saw was a bunch of workers picking up the trash in a park at the crack of dawn. I couldn't sleep because of the time difference, so I figured I'd be the only person up at that hour, but nope. These workers were already out there hustlin'. And what really got me was that no one was sucking their teeth, or bitching about having to be up so early the way you know they would have been here in the States. Every last one of them was focused. They weren't skipping areas, or pretending they couldn't reach certain pieces. They not only cleaned up every square inch of that park, but they did it with a smile on their faces too."

"Maybe they were getting paid triple overtime or something to be out there that early," I reasoned. "It might not have been a normal cleanup crew."

"I thought the same thing," said my friend. "But later on I mentioned it to my wife and she told me that sort of effort is par for the course in Taiwan. Apparently from the time they're little kids, people are taught to perform every job to the best of their ability and without complaint. People grow up with the attitude that as long as they're doing their job well, then they're doing well as a person too. In fact, she said that the only way someone would be embarrassed about their job was if other people perceived that they were doing it poorly."

"Man, those Taiwanese niggas are so fly!" I replied. "They totally get it. I'm not trying to move to Taiwan, but I love knowing that somewhere in the world right now people are picking up trash with their heads held high and a smile on their face."

Now as inspired as I was by that story, I don't want to be accused of trying to paint too rosy a picture. I'm sure that despite my friend's observations, there are still plenty of people in Taiwan who are resentful of their bosses, feel they're not making enough money, or wish that they were doing something different with their lives. No matter what culture you live in, those sentiments are always going to be part of the human condition. But if the majority of Taiwanese subscribe to the belief that they should take pride in and be dedicated to every job, then I know that they enjoy a certain freedom that is still elusive to many of us here in the U.S.

I don't want to come off as too judgmental, because I know there are millions and millions of Americans who hustle as hard, day in and day out, as any trash picker in Taiwan. I do believe, however, that as a society we need to keep reminding ourselves that there is unlimited payment in *every* job we do. We need to talk a little louder about the fact that when you're totally committed to the task in front of you, then you're awake. That when you are doing a great job driving a UPS truck, or being the best bank teller at your branch, or the best dishwasher at a restaurant, even though on the surface you might not appear to have a "fly" job, through your total effort you are moving closer to God. And nothing is more fly than that. Remember to remember that whether you "make" a lot off or a little off your work is ultimately up to you.

In fact, no less an authority than Martin Luther King once said, "If it falls your lot to be a street sweeper, sweep streets like Michelangelo painted pictures. . . . Sweep streets like Shakespeare wrote poetry. Sweep streets so well that all the hosts of Heaven and Earth will have to pause and say: Here lived a great street sweeper who swept his job well."

This is a message I try to share whenever young people tell me they want to follow in my footsteps in the entertainment business. While I want them to have faith that they'll realize their dreams *someday*, it's imperative that they realize that the first step in doing so is to work their hardest at whatever job they have *today*.

For instance, last year I was approached at the Magic clothing convention in Las Vegas by a recent graduate of Morehouse College named Wayne Bell. Wayne told me that he had his sights set on becoming an actor, but was concerned that he didn't have enough money to get an apartment in Los Angeles, where he needed to be in order to go on auditions. "Uncle Russ, I really want to be the next Denzel," he told me. "What should I do?"

"Stop being a bitch and move to L.A.," I replied. "I've seen sixteen-year-old girls move to Italy without a dime in their pocket so they can become models. You're a grown-ass man, so you've got no excuse. Just get on the next bus to L.A., take the first job you can find, and then put your head down and start working your hardest. Before too long you'll look up and you'll be standing in front of the cameras."

A lot of young people might have waved off that advice, but Wayne took it to heart and got on a bus to L.A. the very next day. Once he arrived, he got a job scooping ice cream at a shop in Beverly Hills. And true to my advice, he hustled his hardest at that job. He didn't complain about how much money he was making or act as if serving people ice cream was somehow beneath him as a "Morehouse Man." Instead he made friends with his bosses and coworkers, chatted up his customers, and served each cone with a big smile.

One day he handled a difficult order for a guy who happened to be the manager at the Polo store in Beverly Hills. The guy was so impressed with Wayne's upbeat attitude that he offered him a job. Even though it still didn't pay that much, Wayne accepted it because it did offer one unique advantage: He could also borrow Polo gear for when he went out at night. So even though Wayne still didn't have much other than lint in his pocket, soon he was walking around Beverly Hills looking like

a million bucks. The combination of upbeat energy and looking like he'd "made it" attracted a lot of attention. People
wanted to be around him and within a short time he was able
to make several connections in the film industry.

Wayne would hear about industry events through the connections he'd made, so he started showing up to parties and
premieres, hoping to meet producers and casting agents. Even
though he wasn't on any guest lists, he was able to talk his way
into most events. The people working the door would see this
articulate, positive young black man rocking a crisp bow tie (a
real one, not the fake clip-on kind I try to get away with) and
invariably feel like they were supposed to let him in.

Several months after meeting him in Vegas, I was at the
L.A. premiere for Lee Daniels's Academy Award–winning film
Precious when who did I see working the room but Wayne!
Despite the party being one of the hottest tickets in town, Wayne
had managed to finesse his way inside, where he found himself
rubbing shoulders with some of the biggest names in Hollywood. As I looked on proudly, he managed to strike up con-
versations with such stars as Oprah and my great friend, the
director Brett Ratner.

By the end of the night he'd not only convinced my friend
Mallika Sherawat, the Bollywood star who'd recently moved to
L.A., to let him help her set up meetings with various studios
and producers, but had also struck up a friendship with Brett,
which eventually led to him landing a role in a pilot for a TV
show called *Chaos* that Brett was shooting. When Wayne walked
out of that premiere, I'm sure he felt like the dream that had
seemed so far away less than a year earlier was suddenly within
his grasp.

But here's the thing: Wayne would have never been able to

get so close to all those players if he hadn't been hustling from the moment he set foot in Los Angeles. If he had sulked because he was "stuck" working in an ice cream parlor and handed out cones in a disinterested, distracted manner, he would have never impressed that guy from Polo. And if he had never gotten the job at Polo, he wouldn't have been able to borrow all those nice clothes. And without being able to take off his cap and put on a Polo bow tie, he probably wouldn't have gotten into those parties. And if he hadn't been at those parties, he would have never made the connection with Brett that resulted in his filming a pilot. The chain of events that led to his having a foot firmly planted in Hollywood all started with his willingness to scoop ice cream with a smile on his face.

Wayne's still a young man, but he already understands a secret of success that eludes many for their entire lives: Treat every second as holy. In other words, treat the moments spent scooping ice cream the same as the moments spent talking to Brett Ratner. Whether it appears on the surface to be pedestrian or prestigious, tedious or tremendous, every moment must be infused with love and hard work. There is simply no other way to find long-term success in this world. It's as important a principle as can be found in this book.

GET LOST, RUSSELL

I'd humbly suggest that following this principle also served me very well at the beginning of my own career. Following the unlikely success of "Christmas Rappin'," I was hired by Polygram to promote funk records like Gap Band's "Burn Rubber on Me" or Yarbrough & Peoples's "Don't Stop the Music." It was an awesome challenge every time I took one of the records out to the clubs because at that time most New York DJs were not interested in playing funk. Those records might have been burning up the charts in the rest of the country, but the important New York DJs, guys like the legendary Larry Levan at Paradise Garage or Kevin "Sugar-Daddy" Woodley at Laff's, would always give those records the cold shoulder. They might eventually play them after they'd hit at number-one on the charts, but when I would bring those records around after they were first released, tastemakers like Larry and Kevin were never interested.

Though they didn't say it out loud, every time I approached those guys with a funk record, their body language screamed, "Get lost, Russell." I could just feel it radiating off of them. It got to the point where I used to think "Get Lost" was my nickname as a promoter.

But while getting dissed night after night could have proved very discouraging, I never let those moments get me down. Instead, I was always happy and kept a big smile on my face every time I showed up with a new record in hand. (If nothing else, I was happy that I was at least getting into the clubs for free and therefore cementing my status as a fixture in the scene.) Despite their lack of interest, I would stand there outside the DJ booth begging them to play the instrumental (the vocal mix was out of the question) of one of my records until finally they would relent and give me a spin, probably just so I would leave them alone.

Even at a very young age, I understood that if I wanted to be a truly great promoter, I would have to be upbeat and happy all of the time. I would have to have an attitude where hearing no from a DJ was just as special as the moment when someone finally did play my record. That hearing "come on, you know we don't play funk" was just as magical as the moment the entire club started dancing and suddenly everyone wanted to buy me drinks and be my best friend.

If I could only find happiness in the moments I heard my records getting played, then most of the time I was going to be pretty miserable. But if I could find happiness in the rejections as well as the adulation, then I was going to have a pretty decent career.

THE HAPPY HUSTLER

Whenever you can approach all of your work with a smile and make no distinction between success and failure, the world is going to open up in front of you and allow you to have your pick of blessings.

I know some people might roll their eyes when I say that, or once again grumble, "That's easy to say when you're already the CEO," but I know for a *fact* that you can start at the absolute bottom of an organization, even working for free if need be, and within a few years find yourself running that same organization. If you play your position with an unlimited supply of hustle, selflessness, dedication, relentlessness, and yes, smiles, people are going to smell your potential. Within a few years you will be able to transform from the unpaid intern into the multimillionaire CEO. I can state this with absolute certainty because not only is it a spiritual principle that's taught in all the great faiths, but because I've witnessed it happen. There have been several individuals who started off working for me for free, or for peanuts if they were lucky, and today have more money and influence than I do. Individuals who might have started off answering my phone, but today have me calling them to see if I can bum a ride on their Learjet. Individuals who, through giving of themselves so freely from the moment they got into the game, have indeed been able to get it all.

For example, today we all know Brett as one of the most successful directors in Hollywood, a superstar who routinely earns tens of millions of dollars for his films. Yet when I first met Brett back in the early 1990s, he was fresh out of film school and desperately looking for an opportunity to get behind the camera. I could see that he had a great love for both film and hip-hop, but despite his pestering, I wasn't prepared to let him direct a video for one of my artists just yet. Instead, I offered him what was essentially an unpaid internship as my personal assistant, vaguely suggesting that if he did a good job at that, then down the road I'd revisit the idea of him directing a video for me.

A lot of people coming out of film school would have been insulted by that offer, but Brett didn't hesitate to accept. He immediately started putting the same amount of energy and passion into answering my phone and picking up my laundry that he would one day put into directing blockbusters like *Rush Hour* or *X-Men: The Last Stand*.

And it wasn't easy work—we used to jokingly call Brett my "slave," because he'd work such long hours. It wasn't that I was trying to exploit him, but rather that he appeared so eager to serve that I couldn't help but give him more jobs to do. In fact, another nickname we gave Brett at the time was the "happy puppy." Because that's really what he reminded us of.

After a couple of years of slaving for me, Brett caught the eye of the great Chuck D of Public Enemy. Chuck was impressed not only by Brett's student films, but by his enthusiasm and dedication and let him direct a voter registration public service announcement for PE. Of course Brett did a terrific job, which led to his directing the video for PE's "Louder Than a Bomb," which led to his directing movies, which led to his becoming, without any exaggeration, one of the biggest directors in the world today.

But that initial break only came because Brett was such a great servant. If he hadn't been so enthusiastic about being my "slave," I wouldn't have had him around all the time. And if he hadn't been around all the time, he would have never attracted Chuck D's attention. And if Chuck hadn't let him direct that PSA, while he still would have eventually found his way to Hollywood given his talent, his journey might have taken much longer and been filled with many more obstacles. Instead, Brett's unwavering willingness to serve accelerated his rise to superstardom.

Another person I've seen use selflessness and a smile to catapult himself to the top of his profession is Lyor Cohen, the current chairman of Warner Music Group and arguably the most influential man in the record industry today. I first met Lyor back in the early 1980s after he promoted a very successful Run DMC (also featuring a then largely unknown Red Hot Chili Peppers) show in Los Angeles, despite it being the first concert he'd ever put on. Unfortunately, Lyor's next show, for the duo Whodini, was not as successful and he ended up losing all the money he'd made on Run DMC and then some. Despite that setback, Lyor was determined to be part of the hip-hop movement, so he called me up and asked if he could come work for me in New York at Rush Management. (Whenever Lyor tells this story he somehow manages to leave out the Whodini part. But trust me, this is how it went down.)

The day Lyor showed up at our office to talk about working

for my management company, he walked in on a crazy scene: Run DMC, who I was managing at the time, was scheduled to fly to London that night for a European tour, but their road manager had gone AWOL. Since no one in the office had their passport with them and Run, Darryl (DMC), and Jam Master Jay couldn't go alone, it was beginning to look like the tour might have to be canceled.

When Lyor observed what was happening, he offered to fill in, even though he'd never been on tour before. "Listen, I just came from the airport and I've got my passport right here," he said. "I had a great time working with the guys in L.A. So why don't you guys let me go on the road with them?" I didn't have any other options, so I said, "Sure," and the next thing I knew Lyor was out the door and on his way to the airport.

When Lyor got there, he found the guys waiting anxiously at their terminal. So he walked right up to them with a big smile on his face and announced, "Hi, my name's Lyor. You might not remember it, but we met in L.A., and since Russell can't find your friend, I'm going to be your manager for this tour. Don't worry, we're going to have a blast." Lyor was so enthusiastic that Run, Darryl, and Jay let go of all their anxiety and followed him onto the plane for Europe, where of course Lyor did a fantastic job.

There's a great story from that tour about how the night of their first concert, Jay came up to Lyor an hour before show-time and said, "We got a problem. I forgot all our records." There was no time to go back to the hotel to retrieve them, so Lyor came up with an ingenious solution. An autograph session had been scheduled for after the show and Lyor saw that a lot of the fans had brought their favorite records with them to be signed. So Lyor went out onstage and announced to the crowd, "Run DMC loves their fans so much that they don't want to wait till after the show to autograph your records. Just pass them up to the stage and we'll get them signed for you right now." Then once Lyor had collected enough records, they were able to start the show.

That was just one of the many binds Lyor got the group out of over the course of the tour, in the process completely winning the group's trust and respect. In fact, when the guys finally got back home, one of the first things they asked me was, "Can Lyor please be our new tour manager?"

In hindsight, Lyor's decision to volunteer for the tour might appear to be a no-brainer. It was the first step in forging a relationship with Run DMC, which in turn led to Lyor becoming a full partner in Rush Management Company and earning a piece of equity. Once he was entrenched at Rush, he proved to be so selfless and enthusiastic that when Rick Rubin decided to leave Def Jam, it was the perfect opportunity for Lyor to step in and help run the label. Through his tremendous success as the eventual president of Def Jam, Lyor became one of the most respected figures in the music industry, which led to his current position at Warner Music.

But here's what's easy to lose sight of: Most people, had they been in Lyor's shoes that day he first walked into our office, wouldn't have reacted with the same energy and enthusiasm. Remember, Lyor didn't have an actual job with Rush Management at that time. I hadn't offered him a salary, given him a defined position in the organization, or even a desk to work at. Surrounded by so much vagueness and uncertainty, not many people would have raised their hands and said, "Hey, I can do it."

None of those issues mattered to Lyor. He saw that there was a job to be done and dove into it without any hesitation. All he cared about was having a chance to promote both a group and an art form that he held a great passion for. He had faith that everything else—the money and the titles—would take care of itself.

It's a faith that's shared by all the greats. If you could have seen Sean "Puffy" Combs as I did, when he started out as an intern at Uptown Records, the very first thing you would have noticed was how eager to please he was. If someone needed a package picked up, Puffy was not only going to go get it, but get it in half the time it would have taken another intern. If someone needed to be driven to a 9 A.M. breakfast meeting, Puffy made sure he was waiting in a car outside his apartment at 8:15. If an artist needed a backup dancer for their video, then Puffy would not only volunteer for the job, but also perform his steps harder, and with a bigger smile on his face, than everyone else in the video.

I find it very ironic that today some people look at those old videos on YouTube and like to laugh at Puffy for being a dancer. They can laugh, but the joke is really on them. That's because when you watch Puffy doing the "running man" (the popular hip-hop dance back then), appreciate that Puffy is demonstrating how a true hustler, a true moneymaker, gets down. A true moneymaker shows enthusiasm for everything that he does, whether it's playing the background in a video or starring in it, being an intern or the CEO. He brings that energy, positivity, and enthusiasm to everything he touches.

From Lyor to Brett, and Puffy to Kevin Liles, who went from being a street team worker at Def Jam to an entry-level worker to a marketing director to the president of the company all within a few years, all found success through being invested in every moment. These guys spent their early careers looking for opportunities to be good givers. They walked into work every day eager to serve and contribute, happy to make some-one else look better. They weren't resentful that they were working for free and their bosses were raking in the dough—they only wanted to help their bosses rake in more dough. And by focusing all of their hard work into making everyone else around them better, it wasn't long before they became the boss themselves.

None of these legends sitting on top of the world today were born there—instead they were happy to climb the success lad-der. They didn't think it was beneath them, or a waste of their time, to treat the rungs at the bottom of the ladder with the same passion and intensity that they would eventually treat the top ones. They instinctively understood that if they didn't take their time and get a tight grip onto those bottom rungs, there was no way they'd ever reach the top. Instead, they'd most likely slip and bust their ass.

To put it in another context, you must realize that the day you go into the library and start studying for your LSATs is every bit as exciting as the day you graduate from law school, which is as exciting as the first day you try a case in front of the Supreme Court. And notice I didn't say "treat those days the same," but rather I'm simply telling you they *are the same*. This is what the real moneymakers, the most successful hustlers understand!

So when you see a Lyor or a Brett or a Puffy and think, "I want what they have," understand that you're never going to get that if you only focus on the man or woman you see today. If you want to follow in their footsteps, you must first emulate the young Puffy, or the young Lyor, the hungry and, most importantly, happy hustler who was willing to do anything for anybody at anytime.

SINGLE-POINTED FOCUS

While most of us sincerely believe that we're working our hardest as we move through life, in reality we're often not as focused on our work as we could be. Despite our good intentions, we're constantly having our intensity compromised by a host of distractions. We become sidetracked stressing over how much money we're making or fretting over what the future holds. We operate under the illusion that we are giving everything that we have, but in reality we spend most of our lives operating in a distracted state.

I've certainly been tricked by that illusion from time to time myself. While I'd like to believe that I'm always dialed in one hundred percent, the truth is my effort isn't consistent. I was recently given a harsh reminder of this after I contracted a staph infection in my wrist back in the summer of 2009. In fact, it took almost losing my life to awaken me from my delusion and see just how distracted I had become from my work.

The trouble began after I received anti-inflammatory shots for my wrists, which had begun bothering me during yoga. The doctor made the terrible mistake of using the same needle for both shots, which led to me contracting a staph infection in my left wrist. I've thought about suing, but every time I'm tempted, I remind myself that shit happens. And he seems genuinely remorseful for what happened, so I'm sure he won't ever make the same mistake again.

Of course, I didn't know any of that at the time. In fact, everything felt fine in the hours after I received the shot and I even went to my yoga class that afternoon. But later that night I awoke to the most intense physical pain I'd ever experienced. When I turned on the lights, I saw my wrist was grotesquely swollen, like it belonged on one of the dope fiends I used to see walking around Hollis. (For all you young'uns, the junkies' arms used to get so swollen that their elbows would almost be bigger than their heads.) The pain was almost unbearable. It was like I was holding on to a live wire, but couldn't let go.

The physical anguish was only compounded by the fear of not knowing what was wrong with me. Not only had my arm become disfigured, but my mind had also gotten bent out of shape through worrying about what was happening.

When I went back to see the doctor, initially he was stumped. But after taking some blood and sending me home to await the results, he finally called me back later that day. "Russell, it appears that when you got that anti-inflammatory shot, you caught a very serious staph infection through the needle," he said, his voice sounding very grave. "If you let this thing spread, it could be lethal. You need to come to the hospital right now. Please don't delay."

It might sound strange to say, but the doctor's words actually brought me the first relief since the pain began. With his instructions, I finally had something to focus on: a staph infection. Instead of wasting my energy by paddling in circles on a sea of unfocused worry, now I could fix my gaze on that infection and pour all my focus and hard work into defeating it.

While my girlfriend at the time, Julie Henderson, was freaking out over what the doctor had just told me, I felt surprisingly calm. It was as if the moment I heard I had a serious infection, everything started moving slooooow. Instead of panicking about losing my arm, or even wondering if I was going to die, I simply focused on my job at that moment, which was getting to the hospital. Outside of putting some clothes in a bag and getting into a cab, nothing else mattered to me.

Once at the hospital, I refused to let my focus stray from my task. If a thought came into my mind that didn't pertain to the process of getting better, then I treated it as noise that I had to ignore. The little personal and professional anxieties that had ruled my life just a few days earlier were gone, eclipsed by my intense focus on taking any and all steps to beat the infection. I had been shocked into the present, which was the only place I would be able to beat the infection.

Rather than wait for the doctors to tell me how my treatment was progressing, I decided to take matters into, again no pun intended, my own hands. I called up my good friend Dr. Oz Garcia, the world-renowned healer, and asked him to be the "quarterback" of my medical team. Then with Dr. Oz leading the way, I managed to get several leading specialists on a conference call and had them collectively come up with a plan that would keep the infection from spreading.

Thankfully, all that concentrated effort paid off. With the help of those amazing healers, I was able to beat back the bacteria that were literally trying to eat me alive. In less than forty-eight hours, the storm that had so completely overtaken my life had been drained of almost all its power. Yes, my hand still hurt a great deal. Yes, the people who loved me were still frightened by what had almost happened. And yes, yoga was going to be out of the question for a while. But the gravest danger had passed.

And here's the thing: Despite all the tests, diagnoses, and doctors, the time I spent trying to save my arm proved to be among the most relaxing and calm periods in my life. Through focusing so completely on my illness, I was able to achieve the kind of presence that we all pray for. For all the drama taking place around me and even inside of me, I still felt one hundred percent present and completely awake. It was a beautiful feeling.

Even though it seemed I had "beat" the infection, on my doctors' orders I had to spend the next few days recovering in the hospital while the staff there monitored my arm. Walking around my gigantic room (it really felt as big as one of the suites at the Ritz-Carlton), I slowly allowed myself to start thinking about my "normal" life again.

Prior to my infection, I would sometimes be guilty of dancing around the surface of an issue, rather than delving as deeply into it as I should. But sitting in my hospital room, I realized that I still possessed some of the intense focus I had utilized to beat the infection. Instead of easily becoming distracted, I found that when I addressed an issue on my plate, I was able to lock in on it and stay with it until I'd worked it out. I wasn't jumping from idea to idea, from project to project, and as a result felt very connected and attached to whatever I fixed my gaze on.

Looking to capitalize on this heightened space, I immediately began scheduling business meetings in my hospital room. I met with the entire design team from my Argyle Culture clothing line and, after a lot of intense discussion, was able to achieve a breakthrough on how we wanted to position the brand. I then had a meeting with the Rush Community Affairs Foundation, during which we came up with several great new ideas on how to positively impact people's lives during the recession. After that, I sat down with my partners at UniRush Financial and had an incredibly productive discussion on how to put new research to work at serving underserved communities.

Through actively addressing the work that was in front of me, instead of procrastinating about it, I was getting so much more done. Walking around my hospital room with an IV sticking out of my arm, I ended up accomplishing more in four days than I normally would in a month behind my desk. I might have been hooked up to monitors and had an army of doctors and nurses checking my every move, but through becoming completely engrossed in my work, I also experienced an overwhelming sense of freedom and happiness.

That feeling of freedom is one of the reasons why I'm thankful for that infection, despite the fact that my wrist remains so weak that several doctors have told me I might have to give up yoga permanently. I acknowledge that it shook me out of my stupor and reminded me of what I'm capable of achieving when I'm focused on my job. Now I know that when I'm completely tuned in to the moment, instead of worrying about the past or the future, I can beat a deadly infection. Or design a new fashion line. Or think of new venues through which I can serve the community and find more creative ways to give.

I was always capable of that level of focus, but I wasted a lot of time and missed out on a lot of opportunities by failing to apply it until I had a life-threatening illness. Try to avoid making the same mistake in your own life—please don't wait until you have a staph infection, or cancer, or some other type of physical crisis before awakening from your unconsciousness and truly dedicating yourself to your work. Instead, zero in on what's in front of you today and then *stay* in that zone.

When we talk about operating out of a zone of pure focus and clarity, it all comes back to being The Watcher I mentioned earlier. When I was calmly packing my bags and getting ready for the hospital while my girlfriend was sobbing because she thought I might die, I was being The Watcher. When I was calmly but firmly convincing all those busy doctors to take time out from their hectic schedules and get on the phone to discuss my condition, I was being The Watcher. When I was walking around my hospital room breaking through the creative logjams that had been holding my partners and me up for months, I was being The Watcher.

And guess what? When Lyor volunteered to take Run DMC to Europe despite never having been on tour before, he was being The Watcher too. Just as Brett was being The Watcher when he happily picked up my dry cleaning, or Kevin Liles was being The Watcher when he came into Def Jam every day and did the work of ten people *with* a smile and *without* a single complaint.

I share these examples because I want everyone reading this book to clearly see the connection between these spiritual and worldly practices, between getting rich in the world and getting rich in your heart. I want you to accept that the great yogi, the great athlete, and the great businessman are really operating out of the exact same watchful, connected state. The reason that the yogi meditates for hours on end is so that he can *live* in the same state of consciousness that Michael Jordan is in when he can't miss a shot. So that he can operate in the same state of focus and presence that Donald Trump gets into when he's putting together a billion-dollar real estate deal. The yogi is chasing a lifetime of the clarity that a Jordan or a Trump experiences when he's doing what he does best.

It's the kind of clarity that you may have experienced as well while playing ball at the Y or hearing your favorite song, or perhaps when you are jogging a few miles in the park on a beautiful day. All I'm asking you to do is understand that you can find that degree of peace and clarity in your work too. By becoming more conscious of and connected with your effort, you will be able to feel like a Jordan or a Trump at whatever job you do.

In fact, let me end this chapter how I started it, with a story from Taiwan, one that will hopefully really drive this point home. Remember my friend I mentioned earlier? Well, his brother-in-law, a Taiwanese artist named Wen-kuei Cham, is renowned for creating these incredible one-hundred-foot statues of Buddha that are erected at holy sites all over Asia.

Several years ago representatives from the Chinese government came to Wen-kuei and said they wanted him to design and build a giant Buddha statue that would be erected on top of the famous Emei Mountain shrine in Sichuan Province. Being a very devout Buddhist himself, Wen-kuei was honored to take on the job and spent almost a year designing a special ten-faced Buddha that would be over 150 feet high and sit on the mountaintop.

Once Wen-kuei finished his design, he submitted it to the Chinese officials, who promised him that they would get back to him quickly about when work could begin. Then months and months passed, but Wen-kuei never heard anything. Finally, almost a year after he submitted his design, the officials came to Wen-kuei and admitted that they had tried to have their own sculptors build the Buddha, but they had been unable to master his intricate design. Now they wanted Wen-kuei to come to China to build the statue himself, but there was a hitch: They'd used up their budget on the initial attempt, so Wen-kuei would have to work for free.

Unfazed that not only had his original design been stolen, but that he wouldn't be getting paid to build the sculpture either, Wen-kuei still agreed to take on the project. For the next year and a half he flew to China every month, using money he had raised on his own to oversee the project. When the statue was finally completed, the Chinese government threw a huge ceremony to honor the occasion and invited Wen-kuei. When he arrived, he was shocked to see that his name wasn't on the base of the statue, but rather the sculptors who had failed to execute his design had been given the credit.

When my friend heard about what had happened, he told Wen-kuei, "That's insane! Not only was your design stolen and you didn't get paid, but you didn't even get credit for your work! Weren't you furious?"

"Not really," replied Wen-kuei. "The moments I spent creating a statue of Buddha satisfied me completely. My reward can only be in the process of creation, never in monetary payment. Whether I got paid or credit is immaterial to me. For me being able to make a contribution to humanity through art is all that matters. Everything else is immaterial."

In a nutshell, that's really the attitude we all need to have toward our work. Whether you get a fat check for your effort or get jerked out of years and years of hard work, at the end of the day the payment is always in the process.

But here's the thing: In the end, Wen-kuei did get rewarded for all his effort. You see, despite his official lack of credit, word began to spread that Wen-kuei was the man responsible for the amazing ten-faced Buddha on Emei Mountain. Soon governments from all over Asia came calling and asked him to design Buddhas for their holy sites. While he wasn't that well-known outside of Taiwan prior to the sculpture on Emei Mountain, now he's one of the most-sought-after sculptors in all of Asia. He even recently constructed a fifty-foot "Walking Buddha" for a shrine in India that's being hailed as unprecedented in the history of Buddhism. It wouldn't be a stretch at all to call him the Michael Jordan or Donald Trump of Buddha sculptures.

And that's the point: It's impossible not to do better when you let go of the results. Even though it's not your goal, you're always going to get more, never less. When you are able to lose yourself in the process and stay completely engaged in your work, you are going to become a star at whatever you do!

BEING A

BUSINESS YOGI

Keep your heart in God and your hand in the world.
—HINDU SAYING

Hopefully the last chapter heightened your appreciation for how focused work can accelerate your journey toward enlightenment. If so, now I'd like to take a deeper look at a story that has helped me become even more conscious of the connection between earthly pursuits and the higher self: The Bhagavad Gita.

You've already heard me mention this work (known in Sanskrit as "The Song of God") several times, but if you're like most people raised in the Judeo-Christian tradition, you're probably either unaware of it or only have a vague sense of what the story is about. So before I break it down for you, let me make one thing clear: The Bhagavad Gita is not intended to be taken literally. While the story ostensibly takes place on a gory battlefield, the Bhagavad Gita is not about promoting violence. Instead, it is about mankind's struggle to be virtuous in a world filled with conflict and confusion. As Gandhi once said, "The Gita should be viewed as allegory in which the battlefield is the soul and Arjuna [one of the two main characters] represents man's higher impulses struggling against evil."

Let me also add that my version of the story will probably sound different from most retellings of a holy scripture. The Gita has been retold thousands of times by thousands of different yogis over thousands of years, but probably never like this before!

Now that I've made my disclaimers, let's get on to the story: The Bhagavad Gita relates a conversation on the purpose of life between a warrior-prince named Arjuna and the Hindu deity Lord Krishna. The discussion takes place on the aforementioned battlefield, where Arjuna has gathered his army to face off against the forces led by his evil cousins, the Kauravas, who had forced Arjuna and his siblings into exile and robbed them out of their inheritance. While he is one of the most powerful Gods in the Hindu tradition, Lord Krishna appears in the physical form of Arjuna's chariot driver, having agreed to "coach" the prince during the battle.

But despite having the mighty Krishna on his side, Arjuna is incredibly nervous when it comes time to begin the fight. Not because he's afraid of dying in battle but because he's afraid that by inflicting harm on his relatives, he'll be damning himself to a life of misery. "I don't know if I can fight my cousins," he tells Krishna. "We were very tight growing up. Granted, they've put my people through a lot of drama recently, but I don't feel right trying to kill them. Rather than do something I'm going to regret, I think I should run up to the mountains and meditate about the situation."

Lord Krishna, however, isn't trying to hear it. "Nigga, you a soldier. Your job is to get in there and fight," he tells Arjuna. "You don't need to run away to get your mind right—you can meditate right here on the battlefield." (This is really the epitome of the "moving meditation" I was describing earlier. Essentially, Krishna is telling us that we can be conscious and awake no matter how crazy life seems to be. Even if people are trying to chop our heads off!)

Then Krishna adds, "And as you think things through, remember this—your cousins are evil. By doing your job on the battlefield and chopping their heads off, you'll be correcting their wrongs and making the world a safer and more righteous place."

Then, to make sure Arjuna truly understands the choice in front of him, Lord Krishna delivers the rap that really gets to the heart of the Bhagavad Gita's message. "Look, Arjuna, since you're my man, I want you to understand that you have two choices in front of you right now: The first choice is deciding to be a renunciant. Instead of accepting your job here on the battlefield, you'd rather go meditate on the mountains.

"Now if you make that choice, the choice of nonaction, I'm not going to be mad at you. But I will think you're copping out. I'll think you're not getting everything out of life that you could be.

"That's why I'd advise you to make the other choice, which is to follow the path of action, or 'Karma Yoga.' When you follow 'Karma Yoga,' you're embracing your duty. Every human being has a purpose, or Dharma, here on this Earth. When you embrace that Dharma, your life will be fulfilling. When you run from it, you might have a nice time up in the mountains, but ultimately your life won't be as rewarding.

"If your Dharma was to be a doctor, I'd tell you to go out and heal people. If your Dharma was to be a farmer, I'd tell you to get busy planting some seeds. But since your Dharma is to be a warrior, you need to stop crying and instead get ready to take on the forces of evil. I know you're scared and you don't want to make a mistake, but trust me, you can never go wrong when you embrace your Dharma."

I'll come back to the conversation between Arjuna and Krishna later in the book, but I wanted to highlight that particular section right because it's played an important role in shaping how I view my own role, or Dharma, in the world.

I will admit that over the years there have been moments when I've grappled with the question of whether it's possible to live an enlightened life while also trying to realize my potential as a businessman. Would my work as an entrepreneur be able to exist harmoniously with my evolution as a yogi? Or to break it down even further, was it possible to be what I call a "Business Yogi?"

I've come to believe that the answer is a resounding yes. And the way to achieve that balance can be found in the advice that Lord Krishna gave Prince Arjuna: Don't believe that you have to stay out of the fight and run away from the world in order to be virtuous. Instead, accept that your work can provide service and uplift others. And in doing so, uplift you as well.

I find that message very inspiring as I move through life, and I suspect it will also resonate with many people reading this book. As the Bhagavad Gita makes clear, the key to an enlightened existence is not getting freaked out every time life gives you a tough job to do, but rather through committing yourself to your job while never losing sight of your spiritual evolution.

Maybe your Dharma is in the business world too. Or maybe it's as a doctor, a contractor, a teacher, or an artist. But here's the key and perhaps the hardest part of the story to see: whatever calling you answer to, you will only truly be fulfilling your Dharma when you act as a helpful servant, rather than as a greedy manipulator.

Even though Arjuna's job was to cut off his cousins' heads, in doing so he was actually providing a great service to the world. Remember, his cousins were evil! They were going around stealing land and destroying villages. By getting rid of them, Arjuna was uplifting the lives of his subjects. And that's the allegorical lesson we must take away from the Gita: We should always embrace action, provided it's making the world a better place.

That's why it's so critical that you stay focused on making sure that your work always provides nonharming, stable service for the world. Or to put it even more plainly: Only do shit you believe in.

Period!

IF YOU DON'T LOVE IT, LEAVE IT ALONE

I realize that when I start talking about only doing "shit you believe in," some of you might be tempted to file that in the "easy for the rich guy to say" category. But before you do so, consider that in many ways this is a principle that's actually *harder* for a rich guy to practice. That's because the more money you have, the more possibilities there are for you to become involved in ventures that you don't believe in or don't think will make the world a better place. As a high-profile entrepreneur, I'm constantly getting approached with business plans and partnership offers that I *know* could make money, but I have to pass because they involve products I don't feel comfortable standing behind. Even if it means potentially leaving millions of dollars on the table.

For instance, I'm not interested in selling hamburgers or any other type of food product that I consider harmful. I don't eat that kind of food myself (or let my kids eat it either), so I don't feel comfortable pushing it on other people. As a result, if someone with a proven track record of making money invites me to invest in a restaurant that serves meat, or any product that I think will exploit people *and* animals, I'm going to have to say no. My instincts as a businessman might be screaming, "This is a great deal!" but my convictions are always going to be a lot louder.

As you become more enlightened, you'll have less interest in getting involved in uninspiring, harmful ideas. You can try to sell T-shirts that you know are cheaply made and will fall apart after a couple of washes or mortgages that you know will put people in a precarious financial situation or even drugs that you know will ruin lives, but it won't be long before alarms start ringing in your head. And the warnings will be so loud that it will become impossible to continue going down that path. It will be easier to simply walk away from potential profit than to live with the idea you were only promoting short-term happiness.

Having said that, I can't aggresively knock a professional athlete who signs a multimillion-dollar deal to endorse a fast-food company. For all I know he might have grown up on that type of food and still loves it. He might eat a burger after every game and truly believe that by promoting that product, he's sharing his happiness with other people.

The athlete who I would encourage to reexamine his actions, however, is the one who understands that eating right is essential to success and employs a personal chef to cook the fresh, healthy meals that will keep him on top of his game. Despite that knowledge, he's still willing to get on TV and tell young kids to go buy a burger and fries. That athlete might be padding his bank account, but he could be doing better. His job is to lift others up and help them reach the heights he's already attained, not to load them up with junk that's going to weigh them down.

Whether you are a professional athlete getting paid millions for your endorsement, a recent college graduate looking for her first break, or someone fresh out of jail and desperate for some funds, one of the fundamental messages I want to stress is that making money just for the sake of getting paid is a pedestrian activity that you can rise above. Your focus should be on developing the courage and the conviction to get paid through creating a product or service that you believe in and the world really needs. When you do that, you'll be that Business Yogi I spoke of earlier.

There are some businessmen who can shut off their mind to the damage their product might be causing. They can rationalize their actions by telling themselves, "It's not my concern if these fools are stupid enough to buy this stuff. My only concern is putting food on my table."

The business yogi, however, can't let himself off the hook so easily. He can't cloud his mind to the suffering he might be causing, or to the instability he might be promoting. Because his mind is so clear and he's so sensitive to the suffering of others, he can't talk himself into or rationalize harmful, negative behavior. Instead, he's happy turning down opportunity after opportunity until he finds one that reflects his passion and strikes him as uplifting.

FAKE COKE TO REAL HIP-HOP

Only promoting products that I believe in is a principle I first learned as a young man after I got caught in the drug game. My friends used to sell weed out of their house (their specialty was "Chunky Black" from Harlem for fifty dollars a half ounce), and since I spent a lot of time over there, I used to help out and make a few sales when they weren't home. I didn't feel bad about helping them move it, since I was a big pothead myself. What was so bad about me selling it downstairs if I was also smoking it upstairs? I didn't mind being involved with a service, even an illegal one, provided I appreciated it myself.

Over time, however, my friends and I transitioned from weed to harder drugs like cocaine and heroin. We even got into selling cocoa leaf incense that we passed off as cocaine to unsuspecting junkies (they were using it as part of a cocaine-heroin mix called a "speed ball," which is probably why they didn't notice the deception).

And for a while, selling that fake coke seemed like the best job in the world. I could have all the trappings of a drug dealer—the new clothes and gold jewelry—without any of the risks. It was as if I'd stumbled upon the perfect hustle.

Yet in spite of all the toys I could suddenly afford, when I began to listen to my heart, I could hear that I wasn't comfortable with any of it. I couldn't employ the "hey, I do this myself" rationale, because there was no way I would have ever sniffed some of that fake coke. In fact, I would often go out and buy real cocaine with the profits from the fake stuff I was selling.

Additionally, I didn't like living in fear that a junkie was going to shoot up some of my "cocaine," realize that he'd been tricked, and try to get revenge the next time he saw me. I didn't like wondering whether some local stickup kid, after hearing about me and my boys' operation, was going to kick in our door in a quest for some easy cash and end up blowing our brains out. I didn't like thinking that the next time the cops caught me with a box full of incense they were going to figure out a way to keep me in jail for good. And I didn't like thinking someone was going to shoot that fake coke into their arm, have a bad reaction, and die. Yes, the product I was selling was profitable, but it was also making me paranoid, not proud. Fearful, not fulfilled.

Thankfully, before I could get into any real trouble, I was able to find a greater inspiration in the form of promoting hip-hop parties. I loved that when people came to one of my parties, the happiness they received from hearing a rapper like Eddie Cheeba or DJ Hollywood rock the mic was a *pure* and *lasting* happiness. Instead of selling people something that made them feel happy for five minutes but made the rest of their lives miserable, hip-hop allowed me to give people a high that didn't lead to a hangover. A service that made them joyful instead of junkies. Even though I was only making a fraction of the money promoting parties that I had been selling drugs, my work became so much more rewarding. And, as I began to experience long-term success with Rush Management and then Def Jam, hip-hop became more lucrative than dealing drugs could have ever been.

That's really the beauty of being a business *yogi*: While you might have to pass on some "easy" opportunities, ultimately you will make much more money than you would by just being an unscrupulous business*man*. By insisting on products that provide long-term, stable services, you're going to find that you'll end up enjoying long-term and stable happiness yourself.

This is why it's so critical that you don't fall into the same trap that almost swallowed me up as a young man: just because people will buy something doesn't mean it's OK to be selling it. Remember, people are going to buy *anything* that makes them feel good. Fake cocaine might make them sick and fast food might make them fat, but if it also makes them feel good for even just a fleeting moment, they're still going to buy it. Over and over again. You must look past their willingness to destroy themselves and instead have the conviction and courage to go in a different direction with your skills.

Always ask yourself, by selling this product or taking on this job or accepting this position, will I be promoting short-term happiness that will eventually lead to suffering or am I selling a source of long-term happiness that I can take pride in? If the answer is that you're steering people toward long-term suffering, then I encourage you to look for other ways to serve.

AMERICAN CLASSIC

Despite all the success I've personally experienced since dedicating myself only to products that I believe in, it's still a principle that I have to remind myself of from time to time. For instance, several years ago I was speaking to a group of young people about the importance of giving back through work and providing lasting services. When I was finished, a teenager in the audience stood up and said, "That all sounded great, Russell. But I don't see how selling hundred-twenty-dollar jeans is providing a service."

There wasn't much I could say in response other than "You're right. I need to do better." It was only a short exchange, but it made me really start to think about whether I was doing the right thing by remaining in the clothing industry.

I knew I had to do better, but I also couldn't just walk away from fashion. First of all, when you run a business, you have to keep in mind that it's not only about you. I could have told myself, "That kid was right. I'm going to stop wasting my time with jeans and dedicate more of my time to philanthropy," but then how would that help my clothing employees who depend on me for a paycheck? Who need it to pay their rent, put food on their table, and keep their kids in school? In running a solid business, I'm providing a stabilizing force in people's lives, which is an important service unto itself.

Secondly, while fashion might strike some people as a frivolous pursuit, the truth is I have a strong passion for designing clothes. Fashion doesn't just represent a check for me—it's something I take real pleasure in. Even though I've developed other interests since I launched Phat Farm almost twenty years ago, fashion will always have a place in my heart.

(One of the reasons people might not appreciate the depths of my passion for design is that lately I haven't been comfortable talking about it, precisely because I've felt like it does come off as lightweight, especially in comparison to some of the social and political initiatives that I've become involved in. If a million people are watching me on TV, then I feel I should be alerting them to someone else's suffering, rather than to my argyle sweaters.)

I've begun to feel a lot more comfortable with my role in

the fashion industry, however, with the recent launch of my American Classic line at Walmart. The line features the classic American designs I've always promoted, like argyle sweaters, polo shirts, and jeans. What makes this line different is that for the first time, I'm selling clothes at prices that all people can really afford, as opposed to just some. In the past, I was designing expensive, exclusive jeans that, because of the material they used, ended up costing a few hundred dollars. They looked great, but I felt kind of guilty about it. Today I'm selling jeans at Walmart for fifteen dollars that still look great, but now I feel great about it too.

My goal as I move forward with American Classic is to find a way to bring our prices down even lower while keeping our quality up. If I can do that, maybe I can make the line even more accessible by selling jeans for ten dollars a pair. In the past, I was into exclusivity. That doesn't appeal to me so much anymore. Instead, I want to make sure that no one feels like they don't have access to the type of clothes I would want to wear myself. If you like the designs, which are a very honest expression of what inspires me, then I don't want you to feel priced out.

And while I'm not operating under the illusion that I'm changing the world that much by selling inexpensive jeans and sweaters, I do appreciate that American Classic is a fun challenge that allows me to provide some service as a fashion designer.

What's important to understand is that when I talk about being a Business Yogi, I'm not suggesting that anyone has to stop trying to make money or abandon their worldly pursuits. Instead, being a Business Yogi is simply about adjusting your work so that it becomes less about the bottom line and more about helping people and providing a service. And please remember that being a yogi, whether it's a Business Yogi or any other kind, is a gradual practice. Not every move you make has to be a great leap. Any movement, even if only a small one like transitioning from selling drugs to promoting music or to making cheaper jeans, that is going to lead you toward being more compassionate is a step in the right direction.

A great example of someone I've seen embrace this transition is a beautiful Puerto Rican woman named Veronica who's a good friend of mine from yoga. For many years Veronica was a successful eye doctor in Manhattan, where she examined rich people by day and partied at night. As she entered her midthirties, however, she found herself growing disenchanted with her lifestyle. She was making money and having fun, but there didn't seem to be much more to it than that. She stopped going out as much and started practicing yoga, which helped bring her life back into a better balance. She became so passionate about yoga that she eventually became a certified instructor and even started learning Sanskrit, the ancient language that the yogic scriptures were originally written in.

As Veronica became more and more connected with her spiritual side, she began to take a harder look at her professional life. Certainly there was nothing harmful about being an eye doctor. Still, Veronica felt like she could be doing more out there on the proverbial battlefield. So she made a very courageous decision to spend less time at her practice in Manhattan and allocate more time for people with eye problems all over the world. She began traveling to places like Tibet and India, where she would give free eye exams to monks and other people who didn't have access to modern medical care—people who literally might have otherwise gone blind without her help. When her trip was over, she'd return to Manhattan, where she'd make her money back by doing some eye work and teaching a few yoga courses. She found it to be a very rewarding lifestyle.

After her last trip to Tibet, she stopped off at an ashram (or school) in India in order to receive advanced yoga training. One day a teacher there took her aside and told Veronica she had become so enlightened that there was no need for her to ever leave the ashram. "Don't go back to America," he told her. "You'll just become reentangled in the world. Instead, stay here and live a purer spiritual existence." "Thanks, but I'm nobody's monk," replied Veronica. "I love it here, but I didn't alter my job so I could help less people. I altered it so I could help even more people. I've also got a lot more work to do in the world."

In my eyes (no pun intended), Veronica's response to the monk sums up the essence of what I'm promoting in this chapter: Acknowledge that there's always more work to do and accept that it should always be tied into service.

LET GO OF THE RESULTS

I'd like to wrap things up by revisiting a concept that I first touched on in the chapter "The Work That Prays" and is crucial not only to this chapter, but really to the entire book: Let go of the results.

That means whether you're picking up trash, promoting rappers, or even traveling around the world fixing monks' eyes, you have to let go of the results of your work. At the end of the day, how many pieces of trash you picked up, rappers you got signed, or monks you saved from going blind is nothing more than a distraction. Your only true job is to be awake and focused in the moment. The results of that work belong to God.

This idea of letting go of the results is a concept that I've instinctively known for most of my life, but didn't become completely conscious of until it was explained to me in the Bhagavad Gita.

Essentially, Lord Krishna tells Arjuna that the real reason behind his reluctance to fight isn't his fear that his actions will hurt his cousins, but rather his preoccupation with the results of his actions in general. "Stop asking questions like, 'Am I a bad person for killing my cousins?' or 'Is my success going to be tainted by all the blood I spill?' or even 'Hey, just exactly how famous am I going to become after this battle?'" Lord Krishna commands Arjuna. "Because when you get stuck on those questions, you're getting stuck on the results. Forget all that stuff. Your thoughts should never stray from doing your job with a smile. When you can do that, you're always going to be happy and the results are going to take care of themselves."

Then Lord Krishna followed up that advice with some instruction not only for Arjuna, but for all of mankind. "So once you're done chopping off your enemies' heads, I want you to go back to your village and tell all of your homeboys that if they want to be rich like you, then they also need to detach themselves from the results of their actions. If they don't listen to that advice and start asking about how famous they're going to be or how much money they're going to make, then don't sweat it. Because they're damned fools who should be pitied."

And then Lord Krishna offered a final piece of advice on the connection between work and happiness: "One last thing, Arjuna: Whether it's killing your enemies or ruling your kingdom or handling your household, just keep on grindin' without worrying about the results. If you can do that, eventually you're going to reach enlightenment and you'll find yourself hanging out with me again. Except that instead of standing on a battlefield here on Earth, we're going to be chillin' together up in Heaven." (Though I would add that to a truly enlightened individual, standing next to Krishna in Heaven and right here on Earth are really one and the same.)

Whenever I read that section, Lord Krishna's message stays ringing in my head like a mantra: Let go of the results. It's the most important thing I or anyone else could tell you about your actions here on Earth!

It's also probably one of the hardest principles in this book to put into practice. That's because from the moment we begin to work, we're taught to hold on to the results. When we're in school and we study for a test, we judge our success by the score we get. By the result. When we graduate from school and enter the workforce, we're judged by how much money we make. Again, it's about the result. And as we move through our career, we also look at the result—whether it's salary, title, or material riches—to gauge how well we're doing. We're like Arjuna on the battlefield. Instead of getting lost in our job, we spend too much time worrying about the results of our actions.

But when we can follow Lord Krishna's instruction and learn how to operate as the Business Yogi, the results will begin to seem less important to us. Once we're released from the illusion that we're somehow defined by the results of our labor, then we become free to reach our greatest heights.

To give you a final example, the other day I found myself getting very distressed over a situation with a potential deal. After months of planning and negotiations, at the last minute it looked like my partners might pull out. My first reaction to that news was to pick up my phone and give them a piece of my mind, but after a moment I thought better of it. I realized that ultimately it didn't matter whether these guys cut me a check or not, because I'd *already* been paid. My payment was getting to discuss the deal with my staff, studying the contract, working on the budgets, and negotiating terms. Whether all that work resulted in money or not, I was already rich. I was rich because the effort I exerted had brought me a little closer to God.

So rather than picking up the phone and screaming on folks, I sat with the Gita for a few minutes and then sent out the following Tweet:

> "You have control over action alone, never over its fruits. Live not for the fruits of action, nor attach yourself to inaction." That's a quote from the holy scripture, aka the Bhagavad Gita. Something I need to remember too. I got so wrapped up in this deal, but I just realized, "I really don't give a fuck :-)."

The language I used might have been crude, but the sentiment I was trying to express was actually very pure. The words of the Gita had reminded me that despite our worldly desires, we all already have everything we need in life.

I need to say it one more time: When you let go of the results, inevitably you are going to be rewarded with the toys, whether you need them or not. For example, that deal I realized I didn't "give a fuck" about turned out to be one of the most lucrative of my career! My partners eventually came around and I ended up selling for almost 125 times my initial investment.

It's the same way that by letting go of the results, the sculptor Wen-kuei ended up setting himself up to be one of the best-paid sculptors in Asia. Or how by eventually forgetting about the results and simply focusing on his job, Arjuna became the richest prince in India. So while it is true that you must not live for the fruits of action, when you are able to follow that advice, you're going to end up eating some pretty sweet fruit anyway!

BE REBORN
EVERY DAY

*The world is new to us every morning—
this is God's gift; and every man should
believe he is reborn each day.*
—BAAL SHEM TOV

When I was a young man I did some pretty foul shit.

I didn't mug old ladies, mistreat children, or—God forbid—kill anyone.

But I did deal drugs, run with gangs, and steal from people in my community. I devoured pig's feet, chitlins, and steak without thinking about, let alone shedding a tear for, all the animals that were being sacrificed at the altar to my gluttonous appetite. I even fired a shot (albeit while intentionally aiming high) at a rival drug dealer in a misguided attempt to earn some street cred. In short, I did not enjoy a healthy relationship with the world.

At the time, however, I didn't think there was anything wrong with how I was living. Unconscious of my higher self, I tended to respond to the low notes that were being played very loudly around me. In my unevolved mind, I was simply doing what I had to do to make it on the streets of New York. How my actions affected anyone else didn't concern me.

Thirty odd years later, things have changed. Now I'm a vegan, I don't drink or smoke, and I try to do everything within my power to preserve and uplift life. I run several charities, provide for dozens of employees, and strive to maintain a healthy relationship with the people in my life and the larger world in general.

How did I go from being a drug dealer to a yogi? From a street punk to an engaged, if slightly offbeat, servant of the community? From a kid who spent his days hustling on the corner of 205th Street and Hollis Avenue to a businessman whose office has a sweeping view of Manhattan? From getting booked for selling fake cocaine to writing this book?

The answer is that I changed directions. That I began moving away from my unconscious state and toward enlightenment.

Remember the advice from my teacher Lady Ruth that I shared at the beginning of the book? About how the key to evolution is that when you're headed down the wrong track in life, you must have the courage to simply get up and switch directions? That's all I really did.

Yet while getting up and switching directions sounds simple enough, I recognize that Lady Ruth's instructions can actually prove very challenging to follow. One of the reasons we often find ourselves glued to our seat despite knowing we're headed the wrong way is that we're stuck in what the yogis call the "cycle of Samskaras." Defined very broadly, this refers to the cycle of death and rebirth that all humans are trapped in until they escape through achieving total enlightenment. On a day-to-day level, however, Samskaras evokes our tendency as humans to suffer subtly through getting stuck in the cycle of making unconscious, uninspiring actions over and over again.

For instance, we're stuck in a cycle of Samskaras when we continue to smoke cigarettes even though we can hear our lungs pleading for a break. We're stuck in Samskaras when we head out to the clubs every night looking for a new hookup, even though we feel terrible each time we wake up in a stranger's bed. We're stuck in Samskaras when we keep eating hamburgers and chicken wings, despite being aware of the terrible suffering of these animals before they died—to say nothing of the harm this food is doing to our bodies. We don't love the cigarettes, the meaningless sex, and the meat, yet we have a hard time letting them go.

What makes this cycle particularly insidious is that the older we get, the faster it goes. Time definitely flies when you're locked into a pattern of repeating the same uninspiring activities over and over again. When you wake up in the morning with yet another girl whose name you can't remember, by that evening you almost forgot it even happened. After a while, the uninspiring act fails to make an impression on you. When you keep getting high at night and waking up with pounding headaches, after a while you forget that getting high even gives you a headache. The act fails to leave an impression. If someone who didn't normally get high went out one night, got twisted, and then woke up with a headache the next morning, that's all they would talk about for weeks. He'd be saying, "Man, you won't believe the headache I had after I did some coke." But for the cokehead, it's all a blur. Because when the activities aren't inspiring and stable, they don't make an impression. They wake up with that headache every morning until one day they look back at their life and wonder, "Where did the time go? What happened to my life?" They have nothing to hold on to because none of their actions created a lasting and stable impression.

The inability of uninspiring actions to make an imprint is why people feel like their lives slip away from them. They like to believe that the pace of their lives seems to quicken due to responding to the demands of their career, or raising children, or taking care of a household, but none of those activities reflect the real reason behind their condition. Life only feels like it's running away from you when you stay stuck in the cycle. When you keep making the same mistakes and having the same regrets, it saps your energy, eventually leaving you too weak to take control of your own fate.

IT'S NOT A RACE

While it would be tremendous if this book motivated you to start your spiritual evolution today, don't feel like your transformation has to happen all at once. Sure, it would be nice if you became so inspired that you never smoked another cigarette, ate another piece of meat, or sniffed another line of coke again. The reality is, however, that very few of us are able to change ourselves that radically overnight. Even after you officially quit smoking, you're still going to have days when you want to smoke. You may not have a cigarette in your mouth, but you'll want to smoke, so you'll still be a "smoker." But instead of giving into that impulse, you practice a little bit of resistance and convince yourself to say no. Until one day you see someone smoking and instead of longing for a cigarette yourself, you say, "Oh, wow. I've got no interest in lighting up. That cigarette smells repulsive." When you have that reaction, then you're no longer a smoker. The point is, you don't know when that day is going to come. It could take a week, a month, or it could take a year. You just have to have faith that that day is coming.

It's really about embracing the process of that change. Remember to remember that even when you haven't quite kicked your habit, you will still feel inspired when you pass on a cigarette. Even if you end up smoking three the next day, in that moment you say, "No thanks," you will be reminded that you have some control over your life. There is real happiness in knowing that you can say no, *especially* when you wanted to say yes very badly. As the great sage Swami Chinmayananda put it, "Not doing what you feel like doing is freedom."

There's a wonderful story from the Indian epic Deva Loka about a legendary yogi named Narada that really illustrates the unpredictable pace of evolution. One day Narada was walking down the road when he came across a man meditating. Narada stopped to watch and was impressed that the man continued to meditate for a very long time: It was clear he was working very hard on reaching enlightenment. When the man finally came out of his meditation and saw the great yogi standing in front of him, he said, "Master, since above all other men you know the answer to life's mysteries, please tell me this one thing: How long until I reach enlightenment?" Narada considered the question for a moment and then said with a smile, "Oh, you're getting very close. Only about ten more lifetimes to go." When the man heard that, he became very upset. "I've been meditating my ass off for ten years. And now you tell me that I've got to keep this up for ten more lifetimes? That's not fair!" He became so discouraged that he got up out of the seat he had just been so comfortable in a few moments earlier and stomped off down the road.

Narada just shrugged at the man's protest and kept walking. Soon he came upon another man who was meditating, this time by singing the yogis' chant *"Lokah samastah sukhino bhavantu."* ("May all beings everywhere be happy and free and may the thoughts, words, and actions of my own life contribute in some way to that happiness and to that freedom for all.") When the chanter saw Narada, he stopped his song and asked, "Teacher, how long until I achieve enlightenment?" The chanter was under a huge tree, so Narada just pointed up to its branches and said, "As many more lifetimes to go as there are leaves on this tree."

There must have been a thousand leaves on the tree, but the chanter reacted as if it was the best news he'd ever heard. He started dancing like crazy and chanting God's name even louder than he had been before. Narada smiled and said, "You appear to be very pleased by what I told you." "I am ecstatic," said the chanter. "Now I know there is only a finite number of lifetimes I still have to suffer through until I reach God! Now I have a number. At least I know for sure that I'm on the right path!"

And with those words, having demonstrated that he was truly free of delusion and ego, the chanter instantly achieved total enlightenment and turned into a ball of light. Even though he had started the day with a thousand lifetimes to go, he essentially skipped to the head of the line through that single display of total faith.

That story is a great example of why instead of becoming fixated over exactly when you're going to reach your new destination, it's more helpful to simply stay focused on always heading in the right direction. As long as you are moving away from the distractions of the world and toward that flame of God inside your heart, you're doing fine. Remember, everyone's transformation takes place at its own pace.

FORGIVING OTHERS

Allow me to start off this section with another yoga story, this one by the legendary master Sri Swami Satchidananda that really speaks to this truth.

A long time ago there was a yogi who spent almost all of his time trying to get closer to God through meditation and yoga. He was also a great servant to the community—everyone would come to him for help and advice, which he gave freely, without any expectations.

One day a temptress moved across the street from him and opened up a brothel. Soon there was a steady stream of men entering the temptress's house, which really bothered the yogi. "I'm a holy man who spends all day praying to God," he thought to himself. "I shouldn't have to live around all this nasty, immoral business." He got so upset that instead of focusing on his meditation, he began to spend hours staring out his window at the brothel, trying to give the temptress and her clients dirty looks. Every once in a while he would catch her eye, but she'd just smile and wave at him.

Eventually the yogi died and found himself in a line outside of Heaven's Gate, where he assumed that he would be let in and finally end his cycle of suffering. As he waited, he was shocked to see the temptress in front of him on the same line. The yogi couldn't believe that she was going to get into Heaven before him. "How is it possible that she's not only up here, but ahead of me as well?" he shouted to the angels working the door. "I spent my entire life worshipping God. How could she possibly be more favored than I am?" "Oh, sorry," replied one of the angels. "But while you were spending all that time stressing over what was going on at her house, she was busy thinking about God. Even while she was looking at you!" And with that, the temptress was welcomed into Heaven with open arms, while the yogi was sent back down to Earth to try to get it right again.

The lesson is that we should never get caught up judging another person's actions, heart, or spirit. In fact, you'll actually evolve faster when you look to uplift, rather than judge, those who seem to be struggling in life.

There are many who don't believe in second chances, who want to judge and punish "the sinners." I believe, however, that everyone is capable of taking his or her life in a new direction. That's why I try giving out passes—in fact, I try to keep a pocket full of them!

From disgraced football star Michael Vick to Ashley Dupré (the escort linked to former New York governor Eliot Spitzer), I've embraced and attempted to mentor many people who've made serious mistakes and errors in judgment.

And though I want to encourage you to offer similar support to someone who appears to be moving out of darkness and into the light, I do so with one caveat:

Don't put too much weight into *their* evolution.

This is because often we become so invested in someone

else's transformation that if they happen to regress, we end up losing faith in *everyone's* ability to change. You always want to show people that there is a better "room" for them to enter, but if for some reason they choose to stay where they are, their choice shouldn't shake your own conviction. Whenever I feel like I'm not as forgiving as I should be, I try to remember the story in the Bible where Peter, in an effort to impress Jesus with his compassion, says he is willing to forgive a sinner up to seven times. That seemed like a huge amount of forgiveness to Peter, but Jesus replied, "Man, don't just forgive him seven times, forgive him seventy-seven times." In other words, there should be no limit to our ability to forgive.

So if one of the people I've given a pass to eventually slips back into his or her negative, uninspiring behavior, while I can be disappointed, his or her regression shouldn't make me second-guess my decision to support them. I'm going to always keep encouraging people to move in the right direction. If ultimately they can't grasp their ability to change, that's on them, not me.

YOGA: AGENT FOR CHANGE

I couldn't possibly write a chapter about change without acknowledging the role yoga has played in my own journey from a hyperactive, jumpy, and selfish street kid to a successful, serene (OK, relatively), and compassionate middle-aged man. Yoga not only kick-started my transformation, but has also been the engine that keeps pushing me toward enlightenment whenever I feel myself regressing.

It's a role that yoga has played in the lives of so many people. I'm always struck by how people who have struggled for years with drugs, alcohol, promiscuity, bad relationships, and depression are able to finally find some peace and comfort through this practice. If, as they say, religion is for people who are scared to go to hell, then yoga must be for people who have already been there.

That's not to discount the experiences of those who have found redemption and freedom inside the halls of a church, synagogue, mosque, or temple. Yet each time I walk into yoga I sense an energy—one that I can't personally claim to have experienced in a church or a temple—that seems to make it a particularly fertile environment for change.

It's a unique energy that isn't born out of a specific doctrine or message. In yoga, we are not taught any principles that can't also be found at the core of Christianity, Islam, Judaism, or any other religion. Instead, that transformative energy seems to emerge from a void, an absence of structure and ritual that for many proves incredibly liberating. I've had a much easier time digesting these basic principles when they're delivered without any of the rigidness or segregation that unfortunately come to dominate the practice of so many religions.

Rev Run likes to share the story of how Jesus Christ used to buck convention by welcoming the outcasts—the tax collectors, wine bibbers, and lepers—to dine with him at his table. When Jesus's own disciples questioned whether he should be associating with those sorts of folk, he reminded them, "It is not those who are healthy who need a physician, but those who are sick." In other words, Jesus wanted *everyone* to feel like he or she could sit alongside him and in doing so begin to change his or her life. He didn't want anyone to feel like they were condemned to an unenlightened, unrewarding life.

That welcoming, inclusive spirit of fellowship can also be felt in every single yoga class. It's not an exaggeration to say I truly feel like I'm sitting at Jesus's table every time I put my yoga mat down. When I look around me and see the punk rock kids, the dreadlocked lesbians covered in piercings, the vegan girls with big tattoos of Krishna on their backs, the gay guys, the ex–drug addicts, the skinny black models, the animal lovers and tree huggers, the homeboys from the hood that I bring with me from time to time, all feel inspired and comfortable the moment they lie down their mats.

Be it Jesus, the yogis, Lord Buddha, Moses, or Mohammad, all the great spiritual teachers teach this same truth: No matter what we've done or where we've been, every single one of us can change. Every new day offers a chance for us to be reborn. A fresh opportunity to move away from our cravings and mistakes and get closer to our higher selves. If you've been able to accept and act on that truth through any of those other outlets, then I'm so happy for you. But if you've heard that message before, yet still find that its application is slightly outside of your grasp, then I encourage you to come to yoga. I'm confident that it can give you the combination of faith and freedom that you'll need in order to not only kick-start, but accelerate, your own evolution.

GET OPEN

Another extremely effective way to ensure that you will continue to evolve is to allow yourself to "get open." If you're not familiar with it, *get open* is a hip-hop term that essentially means losing your inhibitions, or letting down your defenses. I think it's also a great way to describe the attitude you should move through life with. You want to always be as open, creative, and fluid as possible, and never become rigid, old, or tight. The freedom you experience when you're open is where all the positive change in your life will emanate from.

Whenever you start to feel yourself become tight and rigid, picture yourself regaining some of the looseness you possessed as a baby. When you first arrived in the world you were open and free—both physically and mentally. If you look at young children, you'll notice how they always open up their chests and arms to the world because they're not afraid of what they might receive. It's only as we get older that we become more inflexible. Our muscles start to tighten, our shoulders start to hunch, and our backs begin to round. Before we know it, we're walking around the world looking and feeling more like a hunchbacked old lady than that young child we want to emulate. Basically, when you're open, you're staying connected to your youthful vitality. When you become constricted and tight, you're moving closer to old age: to death.

Since we all share this tendency to close up, in yoga so many of the poses emphasize opening yourself up to the world. There's the Bridge Pose, or *Setu Bandha Sarvangasana*, in which you lie on your back, bend your knees while keeping the soles of your feet on the mat, and then lift your hips up toward Heaven. Or *Urdhva Hastasana*, part of the Sun Salutation sequence, in which you stand straight as a rod and then bring your arms out to the side and up. Then you press the palms together and, keeping your arms locked, take your gaze up toward your thumbs and the heavens. The effect is that you're literally opening yourself up to the sun, putting yourself in a position to receive all its gifts.

Personally, I try to stay open 24/7 like a New York City

subway station. Not only in terms of my physique, but in terms of my mentality as well. It would be so disappointing if someone came to me with a new idea, or a fresh way of seeing an existing concept, but I was closed off to it because I was becoming old and rigid. I know that miracles are unfolding every day, so I want to be prepared to receive the next great thing the world comes up with. By shutting myself off, I'd just be blocking my ability to change for the better.

Some of the haters will go online and write, "What's Russell still doing hanging out at parties and premieres all the time? He needs to take his old ass home for once." Well, they can kiss this old ass because I'm never going to shut myself off from the world. I can only pray that when I'm eighty years old I'll still be listening to new kinds of music, trying new kinds of foods, reading new kinds of books, and checking out new clubs. I don't ever want to adopt a mentality in which I think there's nothing left for me to learn or enjoy out of life.

Look at my good friend Sean "Puffy" Combs who has managed to stay on top of the fickle entertainment industry for all these years. Since he got into the game, he's been saying, "Can't stop, won't stop." When he first said that, he didn't mean he would try to make hits for ten years and then hang it up, or make hits until he was forty and then call it a day. He meant he was going to keep looking for new acts, trying out new sounds, and finding ways to create big things until they turn the lights off on him. Puffy's been a giant in the entertainment industry for more than twenty years because he's stayed free as a bird. He stays open to the world and has never allowed himself to be insular. It's why he won't ever stop finding success.

Whether you're a veteran like Puffy or a newcomer looking to make your mark, never front like you can afford to shut yourself off from new experiences or different ways of seeing the world. You can never tell from what direction your gift will be coming, so you must stay open to all possibilities. For instance, just because you live in the hood and are comfortable there doesn't mean that you can ignore how other people live. Life might be "good in the hood," but your inspiration might be arriving from a source thousands of miles away. If you write everything off that seems foreign to you as "wack" or "weird," you might never see the inspiration that's intended for you. You might not be familiar or comfortable with the world outside of your experience, but there's a very good chance that's where your gift is going to come from. Don't make the mistake of attracting gifts, but then unwittingly turning them away because you're too closed-minded in your outlook toward life.

The spiritual awakening that's going to lead to your change and eventual enlightenment can come at any second. You could be listening to a certain song, or reading a certain book or watching a certain play, then *Bam!* it hits you. In one second you begin hurtling down the path toward being a fully enlightened being. Perhaps the greatest example of this phenomenon is the story of Lord Buddha. For Lord Buddha, that moment came when he finally ventured outside the royal palace he grew up in. All the privileged friends he had grown up with had been telling him, "Man, don't leave the palace. Why do you want to mess with those nasty peasants? We've got it so good in here." But Lord Buddha didn't want to stay cooped up, closed off from the world. He ignored what his friends were telling him and went outside anyway. And when he did, almost immediately he had that *Bam!* moment. After having spent his entire life shielded from the realities of suffering, as soon as he got outside the palace gates, he saw a dying man lying by the side of the road. In that moment, the reality of the human condition hit him like a ton of bricks. Realizing he had so much to learn, right then and there he set out on a quest for knowledge that would lead to his ultimate enlightenment.

You want to be like Lord Buddha, the type of person who's committed to venturing outside his limited experience—whether it's palace walls, ghetto blocks, or suburban neighborhoods—and being open to the world. So that when your *Bam!* moment does arrive, you won't miss it. Instead, you'll be ready to embrace it and allow it to transform your life.

CHANGE YOUR SPACE

Readers of *Do You!* will remember me talking about Jinx, the rapper I've adopted as my "son." Hailing from the tough streets of Brownsville, Brooklyn, Jinx has already been through so much in his life—he's been shot several times (including in the head), done a li'l jail time, and seen several of his close friends murdered. Yet despite all his struggles, he's never stopped trying to transform himself, never stopped trying to move out of the darkness and into the light. Despite dropping out of school when he was just a teenager, he's managed not only to get a GED, but to earn a college degree as well. I couldn't be any prouder of him.

Yet when I was speaking with him the other day, Jinx was telling me just how hard it is to stay focused and positive on the streets. That every time he felt like he was really changing for the better, the streets would just try to pull him back in with some drama and negativity.

My response was that if he really felt like the Brownsville

streets were holding back his potential, then it's probably time to leave them. Then it's time to move to a neighborhood where there's a more diverse mix of peoples, ideas, and perspectives.

That doesn't mean Jinx should turn his back on his community, or forget where he came from. But rather that he put himself in a physical space that's going to promote his evolution, rather than stymie it.

That's the advice I gave to Jinx and it's the advice I'd give to everyone reading this book as well. You might not be facing the same types of dangers and dramas as Jinx is, but you still might feel the environment where you live is keeping you stuck in a rut, rather than inspiring you to change.

Back when I was Jinx's age, I was starting to feel stifled in Queens, like I needed to accelerate my transformation a bit. So I figured, "Why not move to the Lower East Side in Manhattan?" At the time the Lower East Side was an affordable, exciting, and edgy neighborhood filled with all different kinds of people and cultures. I loved that whenever I stepped outside, there would be no telling who would be walking down my block—it could be a Latino homeboy, an African-American couple, a Hasidic Jew, immigrants from China, or a downtown artist type. I loved that if you walked four blocks in one direction there would be housing projects and if you walked four blocks in another direction there would be million-dollar lofts. On one corner there would be a bodega that sold cocaine in the back room and on another there would be an art gallery where artists sipped white wine. I was so inspired to see all that diversity right in front of me. Even if I never stepped foot in the bodega, or said more than hello to the Hasidic Jews, just being around so many different people and outlooks really pushed my evolution. The energy of that neighborhood served as a constant living and breathing reminder that I was part of the world, that the possibilities were infinite. That I wasn't locked out or trapped, but rather had the whole world in front of me.

Whether you're a black kid in Brooklyn, a white kid in Boston, or a Mexican woman living somewhere in the middle of Idaho, if you feel like you're not evolving at the pace you're capable of, I believe that physically changing your address is a great way to change your mind-set. Even just moving a subway ride away, or a bus ride across town, can help you make tremendous strides in your evolution.

The Lower East Side might not be quite as accessible as it was in my day (almost all the apartments go for a million dollars now, not just the lofts), but there are plenty of neighborhoods where you can still find an affordable yet exciting mix of people and ideas that will spur your creativity and excitement about life. Maybe it's a neighborhood like Crown Heights in Brooklyn, Fishtown in Philadelphia, Little Forest Hills in Dallas, or Long Beach in Los Angeles. Make it your mission to move to one of those neighborhoods and jump headfirst into all the new ideas, attitudes, and cultures that you'll encounter. Not only will you tap into a new source of inspiration, but you'll also protect yourself from getting stuck in the cycle of uninspiring actions that we spoke of earlier in the chapter. Whether it's selling drugs or competing to see who has the best landscaped front yard or obsessing over the local high school football team, when it seems like everybody around you is engaged in activities that you find uninspiring, then you must make it a priority to move.

Some people are so blessed that they can find inspiration in any environment. Whether in the middle of the illest ghetto or the sleepiest town in Montana, they're so focused on their passion (it could be drawing, cooking, writing poetry—anything) that they'd be fine sitting up in their room and getting lost in their passion all day. Most of us aren't wired like that. We're more likely to get caught up in the drama of the ghetto, or become bored to death and aimless in our little town. That's why we must have the courage and conviction to run to the world and embrace all of its inspirations instead of hoping that that energy will somehow find us.

THE SILENCE OF THE SHEEP

One of the greatest obstacles standing between us and our ability to evolve is our tendency to behave like sheep. That's because if you obediently listen to what other people tell you to do, or what other people tell you to think, rather than bringing you closer to your enlightenment, more often than not those instructions are only going to lead you further in the wrong direction.

Our tendency to blindly follow the examples of others is why Lord Buddha instructed his disciples, "Don't just accept what I'm saying out of reverence for me—test it for yourself and make sure it feels right to you too. Otherwise, it's worthless." Lord Buddha understood that in order to achieve enlightenment, we must first awaken from the delusion that all societal rules are good and that our shepherds have our best interest at heart.

Throughout history, we've seen what can happen when people ignore Buddha's teaching and blindly accept what their political and religious leaders tell them. It's that sheep mentality that caused the German people to follow the Nazis and put six million Jews in the ovens. It's that sheep mentality that causes us Americans to remain silent about the eighteen thousand Africans that we know are dying every day due to a lack of clean water. It's the sheep mentality that lets us sit back and do nothing while our leaders kill thousands of innocent Iraqi civilians, or while our corporations become more and more abusive toward our most precious, living entity, Mother Earth herself.

One of the reasons I love practicing yogis so much is that they manage to break free from this sheep mentality. They fall into the tiny minority who aren't willing to be part of an abusive system and instead always look to their hearts for the right answers. A practicing yogi might not talk loudly or go out of his way to make his presence known, but he still possesses the courage of a lion. When the rest of the world is silent about the atrocities inflicted on the helpless, the practicing yogi is going to try to speak out. When the rest of the world turns a blind eye to the nine billion farm animals that are being horribly abused, the yogi will try to suggest that there is a better way. The yogi is always going to love everything and everyone at all times, but that love isn't going to prevent him from trying to change harmful behavior and energy when he sees it.

When you can break free from the flock and start to see the world like a yogi, or really like any enlightened person, does, then maybe you'll decide that you don't want to participate in a war effort anymore. You'll decide maybe you don't want to participate in the abuse of the animals anymore. That you don't want to participate in the desecration of the Earth anymore.

Your refusal to follow the flock could manifest itself in many forms: You could do something as simple as send five dollars to support an antiwar politician like Dennis Kucinich. Or you could do something as involved as becoming an antiwar activist yourself and attend rallies and marches.

If you don't want to turn a blind eye any longer to the abuse of the animals, you could decide to go with Gor-Tex instead of fur when you buy your next winter coat. Or you could make a much more intense choice and decide to cut all meat and dairy out of your diet and become a vegan.

If you don't want to participate in the rape of Mother Earth anymore, you could decide to buy a hybrid the next time you need a new car. Or you could decide that you want to lead a completely green life and actually move out of the city and join a commune where you grow your own vegetables. Then you meet a girl who isn't a sheep either, you two get married and raise your kids on your farm. And then you teach them to have a much healthier relationship with the world than the sheep you left behind in mainstream society.

The point is, any of those reactions are fine. Whether it's a baby step like picking a synthetic coat over a fur one or a giant step like raising your family on a commune, you're moving in the right direction. The level of change that you reveal on the surface of your existence isn't what's important. What's important is that you're undergoing a transformation, be it big or small, inside your heart. That's the change we're looking to promote. As the great guru Yogananda put it, "You don't have to change the world. You just have to change yourself."

What Yogananda meant is that when you start to make this change from the egotistical to the selfless, from the abusive to the kind and from the conscious to the unconscious, the world is always going to notice. The seemingly small or insignificant adjustments you make to your own evolution will always inspire your friends to move in a healthier direction as well.

Not to insinuate that all your friends are sheep, but I promise that after you start meditating, it won't be long before they start mentioning that you sound more confident. Then when you stop eating meat and start being more aware of what you put in your body, they'll start telling you that you're looking better, that you have a new glow about you. After you stop being wasteful and careless in how you treat Mother Earth, they're going to start commenting that you seem more peaceful.

Your simple, humble personal evolution is going to motivate them to change, simply because they're going to want to seem more confident, healthy, and peaceful too. It might not happen overnight, but just like Yogananda predicted, your self-transformation will be changing the world. That truth is why this book is not about anything else but encouraging people to take control of their lives and to have the courage to embrace their own spiritual evolution.

BUILDING BRIDGES

The wise man sees himself in all beings and
all beings in himself. Therefore he never
feels hostility towards anyone.
—Isha Upanishad

Growing up in Hollis, I always thought the flyest cats in the neighborhood were the Five Percenters. For those who aren't familiar, the Five Percenters are an offshoot of The Nation of Islam that are named after their belief that people are divided into three groups: the eighty-five percent who are blind to God and the truth; another ten percent (made up mainly of elites like politicians, CEOs, and members of the media) who know the truth but use it to exploit and deceive; and the final five percent, from which the group takes its name, who know the truth (namely that God is a Black man from Asia), but rather than abuse it, try to use it to uplift people.

While, as you might imagine, the Five Percenters have never found much mainstream acceptance, they were very well-known

in the hood for the flamboyant language and accompanying philosophy they created called "Supreme Mathematics." Growing
up, I used to love to watch the "Gods and Earths" (as members
of the group are known) stand on the corners and "drop jewels,"
their term for philosophizing about religion and the true role of
black folk in America.

While the Five Percenters' silky smooth style of speech
would go on to have a significant, if underappreciated, impact
on the language of hip-hop, I personally never got too deep
into their entire scene. While I loved listening to those smooth
niggas hold court, ultimately I was more concerned with gang
banging, getting high, or chasing girls to spend too much
time thinking about the jewels they were dropping.

Recently, however, I was reminded of just how deep the Five
Percenters really were after I fell in love with a song called "Exhibit C" from the rapper Jay Electronica. In the song, Jay tells a
story of living on the streets ("without a single slice of pizza to
my name"), where he wastes years "shootin' dice, fighting
and smoking weed on the corners / looking for the meaning of
life inside a Corona." He remains stuck in that negative cycle
until he's approached by several Five Percenters, who, as he puts
it, "inform" him of a truth which finally awakens him from his
unconscious state: In life, they tell him, "you either build or
destroy."

As I listened to "Exhibit C" over and over again, I began to
really appreciate the wisdom in the "jewel" the Five Percenters
dropped on Jay. Though I had never thought of it in those
terms before, it is undoubtedly true that through our actions
and our mentality, in life we are either "builders" or "destroyers." The "builders" are focused on trying to elevate not only
themselves, but the world around them (knowing that by ele-

vating others, they elevate themselves). The "destroyers" never awaken from their unconscious behavior and as a result destroy themselves and everything they come into contact with.

In my own life, I've been called a promoter, producer, philanthropist, and mogul. But what I like to consider myself is a "builder." And the thing I love to build the most in life is bridges.

Obviously I'm not a builder in the physical sense (I certainly wouldn't drive a car across any bridge that I'd built), but rather in terms of promoting attitudes, energy, and organizations that help people rise above their perceived differences. I want to help build any structure that allows people to see that at the end of the day, we're all the same. To see that we're all part of the same one God.

If you can adopt this attitude, you'll see that building is such a valuable skill to carry through life. When you're able to keep your lenses focused on the possibilities for bringing people together, you'll be in a position to find success in so many different endeavors. Most people's natural inclination is to cling to perceived differences, so as a builder you will always stand out from the crowd and your talents will always be in demand.

In addition to all the worldly success it will attract to you, building bridges, like all the principles in this book, is also a tremendous way to speed up your spiritual evolution. The more you can engage and communicate with people who seem to be different from you, the more you'll be able to appreciate that we all share the same dreams, the same desires, and the same aspirations. You'll see that the divides between us are much slighter than we perceive them to be. And by recognizing the God in others, you'll be able to better recognize the God in you.

COMING OUT OF
THE CORNERS

In the practice of yoga, many teachers begin their classes by placing their hands together over their hearts, closing their eyes, bowing, and then saying, *"Namaste!"* It's a Sanskrit term that means, "The God in me acknowledges the God or Goddess in you." Our teachers say this in order to remind us that while we might come into and leave class wearing the labels that society has bestowed upon us—man, woman, straight, gay, black, white, lawyer, actress, or whatever—when we sit down on our mats, our practice is to "remember to remember" that we're all connected. That we're all part of the same living, breathing God.

This might sound funny coming from someone who designs clothes for a living, but labels are really something I try to avoid in life. Labels cloud our vision and distract us from seeing how much we have in common with one another. As Deepak Chopra puts it, "When we label or define people, we stop seeing them. We see only [those] labels."

When we can only see labels, we become isolated. Rather than stepping out into the common ground that we should all be enjoying together, we become comfortable huddling in the corners of life with others who "look like us," "talk like us," or "share our values."

When we stick to these corners, we lose sight of our humanity. This happens because instead of hearing all the beautiful, loving melodies that are created when people come together, all we can hear is fearful little men like Glenn Beck or Rush Limbaugh. They're like the greedy landlords of their corners. The longer people linger there, the more money they can collect in rent. So it actually becomes their job to scare the love out of our hearts, to make sure people stay in these corners for as long as possible. As a result, these corners become the breeding grounds for so much of the fear and intolerance we see spreading around the world today.

And I'm not only pointing the finger at guys like Beck or Limbaugh. I'm disappointed in anyone who promotes fear and separation. That includes the African-American preachers who promote civil rights for "their" community with one hand, yet attack gay marriage with the other. While I don't claim to know as much about Jesus Christ as they do, I can't for a second believe that he would have wanted gay people to suffer in any way, or claimed that they didn't deserve the freedom and equality that is the birthright of all God's children. If the folks on Fox or the tea baggers or the black churches really believe that, then they're unconscious of the true teachings of their prophet. This is why I say instead of worrying about "saving" people who are "in the closet," we need to start worrying about saving those "in the corners."

After our ancestors first crawled up out of the ocean, we learned how to walk. Then we learned how to create shelter and grow crops. After that, we figured out how to create governments and societies. Over time, we also learned so much about medicine, science, and philosophy. And in the last few hundred years, we've even developed technology to the point where toys like TVs, cell phones, and airplanes are considered to be as natural a part of the human experience as trees, streams, and winds.

I realize that's an almost ridiculously extreme condensation of human evolution, but the point I'm trying to illustrate is that we've developed so much in the physical aspects of being human. What's now left for us to perfect is our collective consciousness. All the technology we've developed will be worthless, or even worse, totally destructive, if we can't awaken from the illusion that the Republican is somehow different from the Democrat, the Muslim from the Jew, the black from the white, or the gay from the straight. Gently pushing people out of their dark corners and into light is going to be the next one giant leap in our collective evolution.

Having gained more faith that the world always has been, and always will be, in perfect order, there's really not much that scares me anymore. But I am gravely concerned, more for my daughters' generation than for my own, about what will happen if we don't commit to this evolution of consciousness. I know that if people are allowed to continue living surrounded by fear and hate, when they eventually do rise up from their corners, it won't be to peacefully build on our common ground, but rather to destroy it. Whether it's an imam preaching jihad in a Pakistani mosque, a politician spreading fear about immigration on Fox News, or a preacher railing against gay marriage, the energy generated by this fear and intolerance possesses the power to wipe out our presence here on Earth. I don't mean to seem too dramatic, but if we continue to highlight our differences rather than illuminate our common threads, the consequences could be catastrophic. It could be a wrap for us.

Ultimately though, no matter what we do or don't do, the Earth is going to stay spinnin' in the same perfect circles it always has been. The only difference is that unless we all come out of our corners, we just won't be on it anymore.

THE SCIENCE OF SWEET TALK

When we see those we don't agree with huddled in their corners, the temptation is to threaten them, call them names, or even try to move them through force. But if we truly want to coax people out of the corners, the best way to do so is always with sweet, gentle, and loving dialogue.

While harsh, tough words are often the first ones we find on our lips, once they're spit out into the world, they rarely bring back the intended results. Believe me, over the course of my career I've not only spit out, but also been on the receiving end of more mean-spirited diatribes than I'd care to admit.

But even though I've certainly tried, I've never been able to curse, intimidate, or threaten someone into doing a deal, being a better business partner, or, most importantly, changing his or her views. Instead, I've found that I'm most persuasive when I speak to people in a sweet, humble, and graceful manner. That might not always be my first instinct, but it's always my best look.

That's an outlook I wish someone like Bill Cosby would keep in mind when he tells African-American men that they need to do better at taking care of their families and contributing to society. While I actually agree in theory with most of what Bill's saying, there's something about his tone that makes me, and a lot of other African-American men, uneasy. When we hear him say, "Stop being lazy and get up!" his tone sounds hurtful and judgmental. We know Bill is only saying those things out of love, but because we can't hear that love, what he's saying often gets ignored.

Contrast Bill's tone with that of Minister Farrakhan's. When the Minister says, "Get up, black man! You've been down too long!" no one bristles or feels like they're being judged. Instead, when the Minister says, "Get up!" a million black men actually stand up and start crying. They feel the Minister's love and believe he sincerely wants to help. I'm not saying Bill doesn't want to help—I believe him every bit as much as the Minister—

but his frustration often drowns out his noble intentions. The lesson to remember is that when you're trying to change people's minds, no matter how "right" you are, you'll never sway them unless they can hear the love in your voice. Don't forget that the most effective and easiest way to change people is through love.

I realize that's a difficult lesson to put into practice, particularly when you feel passionate about a certain issue. For instance, when I went to the designer Michael Kors's show during Fashion Week this year, I was shocked to see that much of his collection featured fur. Designers like Michael create trends that the rest of the world follows, so I was very disturbed to think that by supporting Michael's show, I would also be participating in the abuse of the animals. Unable to contain my disappointment, I sent out the following Tweet from my seat at the show:

> Michael Kors so talented
> Beautiful clothes.
> Too much fur.
> Kinda hurts to sit thru :-(

Almost immediately, my animal activist friends started Tweeting and texting me to demand that I call for a boycott of Michael's line. My long-time assistant Simone Reyes, who is a committed animal activist, even wrote a blog chastising me for calling Michael "well-meaning" (as I did in a later Tweet). Instead, she said I needed to use my voice to help brand Michael and other designers using fur as "murderers," "sadists," and "cowards."

While I was disappointed by Michael's decision, I felt attacking him and his company wasn't the most effective way of helping him become more conscious of the suffering he was contributing to. That's why rather than call him a bunch of terrible names, I Tweeted that while I know Michael to be a "sweet and talented man," I was very hurt by his use of fur. I added that my prayer not only for Michael, but for the entire industry, was that "these designers will create a trend toward more compassionate choices." I also pointed out that as a designer myself, I know that there are many factories in Italy, France, and Japan that make amazing faux-fur fabrics, which would allow him to fully express his artistic vision without having to hurt any animals in the process.

I really believe that if I had started saying terrible things about Michael, it wouldn't have persuaded him to stop using fur. If anything, it would have probably made him less likely to change. Lots of designers happen to be stubborn by nature, so if they think someone is trying to order them around, they're going to really resist that energy. If I have any chance at awakening them from their unconscious behavior, it can only be through encouragement, compassion, and patience.

My unshakeable belief in the power of encouragement, compassion, and patience is what allows me to have constructive dialogue with people from all walks of life. For instance, I'm often asked how I can go on Fox and have a civil discussion with a Bill O'Reilly or a Sean Hannity considering how much I disagree with them on most issues.

The answer is that if I only use my celebrity to diss people like Bill and Sean, while that might make my liberal friends happy, at the end of the day it won't do much to change their attitudes. Instead, I go on their shows because I believe by becoming a regular presence and demonstrating just how loving and compassionate hip-hop can be, over time I can change not only their attitudes, but the attitudes of their viewers as well.

I especially enjoyed going on Mike Huckabee's show on

Fox simply because he listened very intensely to what I was saying. And I believe his response led to his audience listening intensely as well. I don't think I changed Mike's mind on many issues, but I do think I might have been able to change some minds in his audience through gaining their attention. So if my appearances on Mike's show, or Bill's or Sean's, only end up moving a few viewers out of their corners and toward the center, then I'll consider those appearances very worthwhile.

I'm going to welcome the opportunity to share my opinions with whoever's willing to talk with me, even my so-called enemies. It's never hard for me to do, because at the end of the day, I believe that most people really do mean well. Even those who spread fear or participate in abusive systems. As I always say, if you're truly "right" in your heart, then you'll never have a problem engaging in dialogue with those who you perceive to be "wrong."

FROM ISOLATION TO INTEGRATION

Some of the toughest bridges to build in this country remain those that span our racial divides. We've made tremendous strides over the past decades to address many of the deep wounds created by racism, but there's still so much work to be done. One area in particular where we collectively have to do a better job is in the business world. Despite all the evidence demonstrating that people don't want to be segregated into separate markets anymore, there are too many entrepreneurs, both black and white, who either can't see this new reality or intentionally ignore it because they're afraid of change.

Case in point: Several years ago I launched Simmons Jewelry to great success, yet today I'm still the only African-

American in the mainstream jewelry game. When I recently spoke at a big jewelry convention, outside of the President of Botswana, the busboys, and myself, I don't think there were any other black faces in the entire room. Even though African-Americans purchase millions and millions of dollars worth of jewelry each year and set trends in many sectors of the market, the industry is still almost completely devoid of African-Americans.

Don't get me wrong, I don't begrudge anyone who wants to make a living selling jewelry, provided of course they're not exploiting their employees or Mother Earth. It's a free country and people should be able to make a living however they choose. I do believe, however, that by turning a deaf ear to the mainstream cultural input that African-Americans, Latin-Americans, Asian-Americans, and so many other groups represent, the powers that be are inadvertently choking some of the life out of the industry. It has been so insular for so long that it's started to feel stale, like the air in a house where the windows never get opened. If the industry doesn't open up those windows and let in a cool breeze in the form of some African-American entrepreneurs and designers, it's never going to be able to realize its full potential.

Hopefully the success of Simmons Jewelry will not only inspire more African-Americans to get involved in the business, but also encourage the powers that be to welcome them and their ideas with open arms. Because if hip-hop is the most important cultural influence in America and you don't have no one who understands hip-hop helping to design your jewelry, then you're missing an important element in American pop culture. There's no getting around that.

And it's not just jewelry organizations—any business that still hasn't embraced integration is going to lose a lot of ground competitively. Kids today don't just want access to white America or black America or Latino America—they want access to America *period*. They want to be able to read about Beyoncé and Miley Cyrus on the same Web site. They want to be able to listen to Snoop Dogg and Lady Gaga on the same station. They want to watch *Run's House* and *The Hills* on the same channel. They're not interested in being stuck in cultural corners anymore.

On the surface, this new reality might appear to spell the end of the world for organizations like *Jet*, *Ebony*, or BET, brands that were built by African-Americans in response to the segregation of the past. But rather than pack up their bags and go home, I believe these brands could instead be revitalized by the prospect of chasing the larger market that's now available to them *without* giving up their core. As my great friend and financial advisor Tracy Maitland once said, "There's ninety-five cents in the majority bucket, and maybe five cents for black folks to share in the minority bucket. You do the math." In other words, it's one thing if you've only chased that five percent because you had no other choice. But now that you're out in the middle of the playing field and have the whole market spread open before you, it's imperative that you expand your vision. If you're still passing up ninety-five cents on every dollar because you're only comfortable in your corner, then you simply are missing out on a big chunk of opportunity.

Let me add that it's not only critical to reevaluate your company's relationship with the world, but also your own relationship within your company. I've seen too many young black men and women who've graduated from a Harvard or a Yale fail to capitalize on their Ivy League experience. Meaning that while they were at school, they only wanted to hang out with other black students. And it continues when they graduate and join the workforce; they only seem to want to hang out with other black Ivy Leaguers. To me, that's a problem. They went to school with so many intelligent and powerful white, Asian, Indian, and Arab kids who had something for them. They had money, connections, and new ways of looking at the world to share, but those black kids just ignored it all. They could have been making connections that would have lasted them a lifetime and been the springboard to fantastic careers, but those black kids were more comfortable hanging out with their "own kind." Instead of creating a wide and diverse circle of friends, they chose to limit themselves. What a wasted opportunity!

If you want to find success in this world, you better always be looking to build on the common threads you share with people. For instance, I work with a lot of Jews and while most of them probably didn't grow up around many black people, you can best believe that they always are willing to come to the hood and break bread with black partners. They don't worry about standing out or feeling awkward, because they understand the importance of building familiarity and trust in a relationship.

That's why you can always find me hanging out with my Jewish partners. Sometimes people seem surprised that I spend so much time with them, but I can't see why that should shock anyone. Do you think that David Rosenberg, who is my partner in UniRush Financial Services, doesn't vacation with me in St. Bart's? Do you think that we just do our business from nine to five and then he goes off to his Jewish friends and I go off to my black friends? If you think that, then you're wrong. From the beginning of my career, I've always been excited to meet my Jewish partners or my Chinese partners or my Waspy partners' families to learn about their culture and to experience a little bit of their world. It's strengthened our bond and made us much more effective partners.

So if you're black or Latino and only hang out with your black or Latino coworkers, you are playing yourself! I'm not saying there's anything wrong with hanging out with people you relate to, but you'd better learn how to relate to your Asian boss as well. You better start hanging out with him on the weekends, babysitting his kids when something comes up at the last minute, and becoming a regular at his Fourth of July barbeques. You better open up your heart and make the same effort with your Asian and white colleagues as you do with your black and Latino ones. Because as long as you resist becoming integrated into the mainstream, then you ain't gonna get no mainstream money. You're going to limit yourself to that five cents on every dollar!

Let me also say a quick word about anyone who feels like they're dressing "too white" by putting on a suit and tie every day. When I first started representing rappers, I didn't dress like a rapper. I dressed in a style that I felt would make record executives comfortable doing business with me. At the time, that meant wearing corduroy pants, plaid wool sports jackets with suede elbow patches, oxford shirts, and penny loafers. That certainly wasn't how I dressed in my private life, but that was the uniform I felt would give me the best chance to earn me and my clients some money. After I had become established and had experienced success with Rush Management and Def Jam, then I felt it was OK to start wearing the jeans, Adidas sneakers, and fisherman caps I preferred. But I didn't make that change until I had earned the right to dress however I wanted. Until you earn that right in your career, you need to leave the baseball caps, baggy jeans, and boots at home when it's time to do business. As long as you're in a corporate setting, your best bet is to dress like the guy whose job you want.

Look, there's no doubt that in the past African-Americans and other minorities were limited by markets built on fear and segregation. That market, and that America, are dead now. To be successful moving forward, African-American entrepreneurs must let go of that past and stay focused on the unlimited opportunities now in front of them. Again, if you're an entrepreneur and can't step out of those old corners, then you won't be stepping into any new money either. It's that simple.

A NEW SPACE

One of the reasons I wanted to launch the Global Grind Web site was because I saw the Internet as a space where the baggage of the past would get checked at the door and the hip-hop generation would be free to build a community that reflected its belief in diversity and acceptance. Yet the more active I've become online, the more apparent it's become that not only are the old racial walls being rebuilt in cyberspace, but many of the builders are actually African-American. It's very disappointing because if African-Americans are building anything on the Internet it should be bridges, not walls. Yet every time I go online and check out the popular black Web sites, I feel like I see another wall slowly being put in place.

I see these walls being built when a black Web site starts off a story about Tom Cruise by saying, "Now, in white folks' news . . ." I see walls being built when a site exclusively refers to white women as "Beckys" (after a popular, though hardly complimentary, rap song about white women). Just as I see a wall being built when a Web site has a weekly feature called, "White Folks Do the Darnedest Things."

But where I see these walls going up most clearly is in many African-American sites' obsession with interracial dating, or as they like to call it, "swirling" (after those black-and-white ice-cream cones). Every time a Halle Berry or a Serena Williams or, yes, a Russell Simmons goes out to dinner with someone who isn't black, these sites are quick to post a "swirl alert" with a picture of the "offending" couple underneath.

While these "swirl alerts" may be intended to be humorous, the comments they generate reveal that too many African-Americans still view interracial romance as though it is some sort of crime or affront to our community. For example, after Bossip.com ran a picture of me and my blond-haired, blue-eyed then-girlfriend Julie Henderson under the headline, "Digging for Gold," the story generated some very hurtful comments. Even one that went as far to suggest that my "preference" for white women indicates that I must have hated my late mother.

Comments like that are pretty intense, but ultimately I can't help but laugh when I read them. As I teasingly wrote in an open letter to Bossip in response to all their "swirl" posts, "Before yoga and marriage, back in the *Krush Groove* days, I was fat and high on coke, but I was still known to have the baddest girls from all over the world. Now I'm rich, vegan, sober, and in much better shape . . . Can't u guys just accept that my game is tight?!!!!"

And for the record, let me add that while I've certainly dated plenty of white women, I've also dated plenty of Asian, Indian, Puerto Rican, and, yes, African-American women as well. So if I do have a preference, it's not for a particular race, but rather for attractive, funny, charming, non-cigarette-smoking, non-animal-eating, non-fur-wearing women who can talk about yoga with me!

These sites can write whatever headlines they want, but they should know that I've never lost a moment's sleep worrying about whether people will think I'm a "coon" or a "sell-out." I've never second-guessed any of my romantic choices because of race, just as I've never felt threatened by the choices Halle Berry, Stacey Dash, Sanaa Lathan, or any other sister has made. I see them as part of a new America and I'm happy to share it with them.

It's a new America that I'd like to urge the so-called white pop sites to be more active in acknowledging as well. For instance, as I'm writing this, the unquestioned queen on all the "black" sites is Nicki Minaj. You can't go to one of them without reading about what Nicki wore in her last video, what she did to her hair, or what she said about someone else. She's all over those sites. But up until MTV finally picked her up for their VMA pre-show, Nicki couldn't seem to get arrested on some of these "white" sites. It seems the only black stars those sites want to acknowledge are those like Will Smith or Jay-Z who have risen to heights so high they can't be ignored anymore. Those sites could be creating black stars and making themselves cutting edge, but instead they're only reacting to black stars, which is very dull. The cultural gatekeepers at those sites don't understand that their readers are interested in exciting emerging stars of all races, colors, sexes, and orientation. They're not interested in a steady diet of the same old thing. So any pop sites that are slow to acknowledge what's happening in black America are just revealing that their taste buds aren't working right.

And really, no matter what field you're in, if you're building cultural walls, be it intentionally or unconsciously, you're going to lose. Anyone who looks to keep people apart rather than bring them together is swimming against a very strong tide.

ANY NAME WILL DO

Out of all the bridges we can construct, none will do more to lift our collective consciousness than those that aim to bring together the world's religions. While the idea of creating a lasting connection between Christians and Jews, or Muslims and Hindus, might seem daunting to some, I've always felt that such bridges should be among the easiest to build. That's because while I'm certainly no scholar, even I can see that all the world's great religions run parallel. Their scriptures might have been written in different languages by men of different colors during different eras, but at their essence, they all revolve around the same truth: Our only purpose here on Earth is to achieve union with God.

I caught a glimpse of what is possible when we attempt to build on our spiritual connections when, during the summer of 2009, as president of the Foundation for Ethnic Understanding (FFEU), I helped host a group of twenty European imams and rabbis visiting America as part of a "twinning" program. The idea behind the trip was that by having top rabbis and imams from the same European cities become "twins" and visit America together, they could begin to create a connection that would bridge the mistrust that, despite their physical proximity, is perceived as separating their faiths.

For that particular trip, Rabbi Marc Schneier, my good friend and partner in the FFEU, selected imams and rabbis from cities that have seen a troubling rise of both anti-Semitism and Islamophobia in recent years, including London, Paris, Moscow, and Geneva. For four wonderful days, these men set aside their emotional and political baggage and focused on exchanging ideas with individuals who, in a different setting, might have been considered adversaries.

One of the highlights of the trip was a visit to New York City, where the group met with Mayor Bloomberg and visited the United Nations. While at the UN, I gave a short speech to my new friends, applauding their open-mindedness and noting how encouraging it was to see them talking, laughing, and breaking bread together. In closing, I shared a passage from the Bhagavad Gita in which Arjuna asks Lord Krishna how he can be sure that he's properly honoring him. "Whether you know me as Krishna or not is unimportant. As long as you are living by these codes and are practicing Karma yoga, you will still come to me," responded Lord Krishna. As I explained to the imams and rabbis, that passage serves as a reminder that the label you affix to your relationship with God isn't that important. What matters is that your actions are non-harming, uplifting, and humble. As long as you can live in that spirit, you'll always be moving toward God, no matter what religion you align yourself with.

After my speech the imam from Geneva called me over and explained that he had been very inspired by Lord Krishna's words. He told me that there is an almost identical passage in the Koran and that in appreciation of that message he wanted to give me a special pair of *misbaha*, or Muslim prayer beads.

It was a wonderful gesture, especially since I'm something of a prayer bead junkie. I keep a huge collection of beads in the yoga room I've set up in my apartment, including Catholic rosaries, Tibetan Buddhist beads, Hindu prayer beads, Zen Buddhist beads, and now the imam's *misbaha*. It's gotten to the point that I don't even know how many beads I have anymore.

And as I told the imam from Geneva, when it comes to prayer beads, I don't discriminate. When it's time to meditate, I could just as easily snatch up a Hindu pair as the Catholic rosaries. To me, prayer beads are prayer beads. What religion they represent, or what temple they came from, is irrelevant to me. My only concern is whether or not they help me get closer to God.

I suspect that God feels the same way. Let's say hypothetically that one day I picked up a pair of Catholic rosaries and began meditating and found myself in one of the most intense states of meditation I'd ever experienced. Instead of meditating for half an hour, I kept counting those beads and chanting God's name for hours and hours. To the point where I was actually approaching a state of enlightenment.

Does anyone really believe that God, upon noticing me drawing closer and closer, would think, "Hold on a second. Russell isn't Catholic, so why is he using rosaries to help him meditate? That's no good. I'm going to have to shut this down." How insane does that sound? I don't claim to have too much insight into God's thought process, but I am fairly confident that if one day I am able to achieve such a miracle, God won't care what sort of prayer beads I used to get there. He'd just be pleased that I'd lived up to my potential.

Anyone who believes that God cares more about our path than our destination must not have read any of the great scriptures. A Christian who thinks that one billion Hindus aren't going to be able to get into Heaven because they don't pray to Jesus Christ by name has not read his Bible correctly. Just as a Hindu who thinks that Lord Krishna doesn't love righteous, compassionate Muslims is living in ignorance as well. That Hindu might have turned the pages of the Bhagavad Gita, but evidently he did not truly digest Lord Krishna's words.

We must accept that all the scriptures are just tools, spiritual apparatus designed to help us reach a single destination: enlightenment. Once we arrive at enlightenment, we can throw out our Bibles, our Bhagavad Gita, our Korans, or whatever books helped us achieve that state, as they've served their purpose. It's as if the scriptures are ladders we can use to climb up a mountain. Once we've reached the summit, we can kick those ladders back down to the valley for someone else to use. We don't need them anymore because once you reach enlightenment, there's no going back.

As you've certainly noticed by now, I'm open to employing any of these spiritual tools if I feel they will help me get a little bit closer to God. If rosaries can help move me away from my ego and closer to God, then I'm going to count the shit out of them. If a "jewel" from a Five Percenter feels like it can help me move even a few more inches in the right direction, then I'm going to clutch that jewel too. And if I feel like the words of the yogis can pick me up and carry me even closer to my goal, then I'm going to keep reading the Yoga Sutras until it's part of my essence. Religion is like running water to an ocean. We only travel on it in order to reach that sea of God.

Remember, the purpose of this book is not to "convert" you to yoga, or to convince you to put down the Bible in favor of the Yoga Sutras. All that I ask is that you leave these pages with a newfound tolerance for the messages found in all of the great scriptures, whether they're part of your life or not. In a world where there's definitely a scarcity of it, we can never have enough tolerance and compassion.

I'll concede that promoting tolerance over fear and rigidness can be daunting. Even the relatively simple act of convincing a dozen imams and rabbis to come together under the same roof felt Herculean at first. It took months of cajoling to convince these men that real progress could be made through talking and traveling together. However, once we finally got them in the same room and they could see just how much they had in common, we were actually able to bridge the disconnect very quickly. It was particularly encouraging to watch the imam and rabbi from Paris build a strong relationship. Coming into the program there was no connection between them, but after a few days they were literally walking arm in arm. In fact, they almost got along too well because they started spending so much time together that they didn't really connect with the rest of the delegation. I'm not mad at them, though, because they continued working together when they got back to France and have currently set up more than eighty events where rabbis speak to mosques and imams speak to synagogues. In a country where there's so much anti-Semitism and Islamophobia, that's such important work. It was inspiring to see that the program truly had the most success in the places where it was needed the most.

Whenever I start to feel like building bridges is too difficult, or that they will never lead anywhere, I always try to remember this: Bringing people together isn't a luxury, but rather an essential component to our spiritual well-being. That's because without bridges connecting us, we become isolated. And isolation is a very virulent form of sickness.

Conversely, building the bridges that bring people together is going to keep you healthy—both spiritually and financially. Whether it's bringing together imams and rabbis or investors and innovators, when you are the person who constructs the bridge, you will be rewarded. You are going to attract their love, their respect, and, yes, their money. Your open, loving, and inclusive attitude is going to serve you very well in every facet of your life.

ACCEPTANCE IS
THE ANSWER

*Do thy work, O Winner of wealth, abandoning
attachment, with an even mind in success and failure,
for evenness of mind is called yoga.*
—BHAGAVAD GITA

While I'm certainly humbled by the successes I've experienced over the years, my goal moving forward is not to
rack up any more accomplishments, or even to avoid making
any more mistakes. Instead, my focus is on always trying to
treat the inevitable highs and lows of life with the same blissful,
calm energy.

For a long time now, I haven't been interested in hosting
celebrations. I work in an industry where, whether it's a new
album, clothing line, restaurant, birthday, or farewell, any excuse to throw a party always sounds like a good one. But outside of hosting charity events, which I'm happy to do, I've lost

my desire to celebrate what are perceived as accomplishments. As I like to say, "What are you left with after a celebration? A hangover."

At first I couldn't figure out why I'd grown so uninterested in the prospect of celebrating a birthday, the launch of a new project, or even the holidays. I started to wonder, "Am I just getting old and grouchy?" But now I realize that it's a natural part of my spiritual evolution. This is because one of the by-products of moving toward a more enlightened state is that you will not get too excited about "good news," or too down about "bad news." It's a critical step in your evolution, because when you can learn to smile at *all* of life's adventures, the roller-coaster ride that is life will leave you exhilarated and shouting for more, rather than nauseous and scrambling to get off.

While my inspiration used to be the guys who would throw the biggest parties, now it's become the individuals who are much more calm and balanced in their relationship with the world. The individuals who are so enlightened that they act the same way at celebrations as they do at funerals. Whether they're watching a young child unwrapping gifts or an old man being lowered into the ground, someone who's Super Rich is going to radiate the same calm, blissful energy. In fact, I've heard about some yogis who won't go to funerals because they know that their blissful smile might be misinterpreted. And since an enlightened being knows his only job is to relieve the suffering of others, rather than unintentionally offend a griev-ing relative, he just stays home.

One day I hope to be as blissed out as those enlightened individuals, but for now I'd be happy if I could reach the level of enlightenment that I've witnessed in a young child I've semi-adopted and grown to love dearly named Jasmine. When I first met Jasmine, she'd already been in and out of the hospital countless times as she struggled with HIV/AIDS. But despite all the obstacles she's faced, and all her near-death encounters, Jasmine is a fighter. She's never allowed her sickness to dull her enthusiasm and appetite for life.

About a year ago Jasmine landed back in the hospital with a serious infection and soon after called to ask if I could send her a laptop computer. Confined to a hospital bed for most of the day, she simply wanted to be able to surf the Web and watch videos. Of course I said yes and a few days later Jasmine called to thank me. When I took Jasmine's call, I had been stewing over a business deal I thought was unfair, but the moment I heard her upbeat, happy, and loving voice, all the negativity was washed out of my mind. As she rattled off the music she'd been able to listen to and the Web sites she'd visited, I don't think I'd ever heard anyone so genuinely appreciative about a gift. If I hadn't known she was calling from a children's hospital, it would have been impossible to guess that this little girl was going through an ordeal that would make even the strongest of us miserable, resentful, and depressed. Hearing her beautiful spirit pour through the phone reminded me to stop getting so caught up in my trivial "problems" and instead refocus on just how blessed I've been.

Thankfully, I get these wake-up calls often. Just the other day I was complaining about how my wrist was still bothering me and affecting my yoga practice. Complaining about how hard it was for me to go through the poses while protecting my wrist and how I just wished that I could have two good wrists like everyone else.

When I made it to class that afternoon, a young woman sat down on a mat beside me and unscrewed a prosthetic leg. As I watched in amazement, she proceeded to go through the entire class while practicing on her knees, smiling and breathing in every pose despite her physical limitation. Watching her accept her limitations with such gracefulness, I found that the sore wrist I had been complaining about only a few hours earlier immediately began to feel better and be less of a burden.

Whenever I see Jasmine in the hospital or that one-legged yogi in class, I am reminded of a critical truth taught by Lord Buddha: While pain is inevitable, suffering is optional. That's not to make light of what those two brave souls have gone through, but rather to suggest that despite their pain, they are not suffering. Their bodies may be compromised, but their spirits are robust. Their pain has purified them, washed wasteful emotions like anxiety, envy, and regret right out of their systems.

Jasmine and the one-legged yogi (I've since learned her name is Margaret) are living testaments to the truth that no matter what sort of "obstacles" life throws in your path (and hopefully none of them will be as challenging as living with HIV or losing a limb), it is possible to operate out of a state of acceptance. That while we can't avoid the pain that accompanies the human existence, it is possible to avoid the suffering that overwhelms so many people's lives.

I witnessed possibly the most dramatic example of this truth during a recent trip I took back to Hollis with a group called Bury Da Beef. The organization was started by the activist Erica Ford with the mission of helping educate young people and provide them with an alternative to the deadly gun culture that not only plagues Hollis, but neighborhoods all over this country.

While in Hollis, we met with numerous parents who'd lost their children, including my old friend Jelly Red, who spoke so movingly of his son Chris. His eyes welling up with tears, Jelly told us that even years after Chris's murder he still thinks about his son every day.

As a parent, I can barely fathom the terrible pain that must result from losing a child. Yet as these courageous mothers and fathers spoke, I was struck how, despite their loss, they were able to display such poise and grace. There were still plenty of tears, but there was also an overwhelming sense of strength and purpose.

These parents weren't out there on the street meeting with activists in order to save their children—it was already too late for that. They were there to save someone else's child. They were there to hug another mother, or grip the shoulder of another father who'd also gone down the terrible path they had been forced down.

You see, the only way for these parents to relieve their suffering was to help relieve the suffering of someone else. Through finding someone else in pain and simply hugging them. Not because they needed a hug, but because they needed to *give* a hug. They had been forced into realizing a critical truth: What you do for others will happen for you. That's the only way to lessen such a terrible burden.

What I hope to demonstrate in this chapter is that through practicing acceptance, it is possible to let go of much of the needless anger, disappointment, and regret that many of us carry through life. Through constantly wanting things to be different—our careers, our love lives, our finances, our bodies, and our relationships with the world—we unintentionally impede our own progress. In fact, it could be said that needing things to be different is the cause of *all* suffering. In the ancient Hindu scriptures it is written that "even the desire for liberation is a bondage."

That's why if each of us could apply even just a fraction of Jelly Red's, Margaret's, or Jasmine's unwavering acceptance to the perceived challenges of our own lives, we would be so blessed. We would be able to see that far from being a harsh and hurtful space trying to trip us up, ours is actually a sweet and loving world looking to lift us up.

NO REGRETS

Whenever I'm interviewed, one question I always seem to get is, "What are your biggest regrets?" It's a fair question, since even though I've experienced plenty of success, I've also been involved in plenty of situations that the world might label "failures."

Yet despite all the worthy candidates, every time someone asks that question, my mind starts to spin like a disc that won't play. I'm always at a loss for words because the truth is that I don't have many regrets. It's not that I think I'm flawless, or haven't gone down plenty of wrong paths, but rather that I try to accept every disappointment I've had—be it professional, personal, or physical—as a learning experience.

To give an example: For a long time, if I would cop to one mistake, it would probably be "losing" the Beastie Boys. For those of you unfamiliar with the story, the Beastie Boys, comprised of MCA, Mike D, and Ad-Rock, were a trio of white rappers from New York City and one of the first acts that Rick Rubin and I signed to Def Jam Records. Their debut album *License to Ill* was one of the most successful in the label's history, landing at number one on the Billboard album chart (a first for a hip-hop album) and selling more than nine million copies. But in the aftermath of the album's success, the strong bond that had been built between Rick and me and the Beasties began to fray.

After the Beasties finished touring in support of *License to Ill*, the guys just wanted to chill and bask in their success for a minute. Rick and I, however, had other ideas. Since the Beasties were red-hot, we wanted to get them back into the studio as quickly as possible and capitalize on their popularity. Ultimately we all wanted the same thing—for the Beasties to make the best music they were capable of and to reach the largest possible audience—but there was a serious difference of opinion on how to get there. To complicate matters even more, the Beasties also wanted a lot of money up front before they would begin work on the new album. All that drama drove a wedge between us and eventually the Beasties decided to leave Def Jam for what they believed to be a sweeter deal with Capitol Records.

For many years, I held on to a lot of pain about the breakup. Besides being one of the acts that helped put Def Jam—and hip-hop—on the map, the Beasties were like my little brothers. We'd grown up touring, partying, and making music together. Outside of the professional considerations, losing their friendship for a period (we're all cool again now) was a tough blow.

But looking back at the situation, I can accept that I didn't lose nothin', because the Beasties were never mine to "lose." I can now see that the split was just proof of how the world is already in perfect order. When the Beasties went to Capitol, they were given a big suitcase full of cash and told to take their time making their next album, which was exactly what they needed at that point in their career. They ended up dropping *Paul's Boutique*, an album that is still hailed as one of the most influential in pop history almost twenty-five years later.

Things didn't turn out too badly for Def Jam either. Though

"losing" the Beasties was seen by many at the time as a blow to our brand, Def Jam went on to enter one of its most successful phases, signing superstars like Jay-Z, Warren G, DMX, and Ludacris and cementing its status as the preeminent label in hip-hop.

That's why today if someone asks me about the Beastie Boys, while I'll humbly admit to having stumbled in that situation, I won't admit to having any regrets. We were kids back then and were equally stupid, stubborn, and shortsighted. If I still regretted the Beastie Boys leaving Def Jam, that would mean that I also regretted all of their subsequent success as well. Which of course I don't. I love that the Beastie Boys are still inspired and relevant twenty-five years later, just as I still love to put on *License to Ill* and get the same rush I did back in the 1980s. Instead of regretting any of it, I accept all of it: the wild successes and the disappointments, the incredible camaraderie and resentful breakups. I accept that all of it was necessary in order to rest in the perfection that is our lives today.

TEACHABLE MOMENTS AND TEMPER TANTRUMS

I've found that the most effective way for me to move past the obstacles of the world is by turning inward and accepting my imperfections. Doing so allows me to rest in a more peaceful place, both in my head and in my heart. It also allows me to accept the imperfections of those around me, which makes me a much better partner, in both my professional and personal life.

This is why whenever I speak to young people, I always tell them, "If a teacher corrects you in front of the class, don't get defensive or embarrassed. Instead, say, 'Thank you.'" Acknowledge that that correction is a blessing, what could be called a "teachable moment." The perception might be that you've lost something—face, or cool points, or respect—by being publicly corrected, but the reality is you just got blessed.

We waste so much time in life worrying about being labeled a "loser" or "weak" or simply as being "wrong." Instead of falling into that trap, focus on accepting any and all lessons that make us stronger. The student will do better on his next test after being corrected by his teacher. The employee will do better for his company after being reprimanded by his boss. And so on and so on.

This lesson is particularly relevant for people who come from what I call a "street" background. Those of us who grew up on the "street" (which could mean a trailer park as easily as a housing project) were conditioned to believe that any correction or reprimand was a personal affront. A lot of you folks are familiar with the type of mentality I'm talking about. It's a macho (though plenty of women practice it too) philosophy that instructs us to view almost every disagreement as a battle that must be won, every perceived wrong as something that must be righted. And I can't knock someone who's grown up in the ghetto, or in a trailer park, or in any proximity to destitution and despair, for feeling that way. The combination of poverty, addiction, and violence that is found on the streets does often make it feel like a dog-eat-dog world, a world where you've got to fight back or end up as someone's lunch.

The truth is, however, that this *isn't* a dog-eat-dog world. Instead of feeling like you have to snarl when you see another dog coming down the street, you can wag your tail instead. No matter where you live and what challenges you face, please understand that loving, sweet, and gracious acceptance is always the best response to every situation. You don't have to "keep it real," or worry about "playing yourself" whenever you feel challenged. Instead, the best response is always to say "thank you" when you're corrected, "I'm sorry" when someone screams on you, and "I love you" when you're challenged. Reacting that way doesn't make you a "punk," or a "bitch," or a "sellout." Instead, it makes you a yogi, which is one of the best things you can be in life.

I know from firsthand experience that even after years of spiritual practice, it can still be very hard to completely let go of that street mentality. A few summers ago, I went out for brunch in the Hamptons with my daughter Ming Lee and a friend of mine, enjoying a nice meal of organic smoothies and vegan French toast (doesn't sound too street, right?). After paying the bill, we were crossing the street to go back to my car when our waitress came running out after us, yelling that I had forgotten my credit card. When she caught up to us, in addition to giving me my card, she also handed me a demo that her cousin had made and asked if I would listen to it. Now in the Hamptons, the law is that when pedestrians are in a crosswalk—which we were—traffic has to stop and wait for them to cross. That meant the whole time I was talking to the waitress, I was also holding up traffic. The driver of the first car in line was growing more and more impatient, but I was oblivious to his suffering. Finally the driver reached his boiling point and, sticking his head out his window, screamed at me, "Hey, you son of a bitch! Get the hell out of the road!"

I was enraged that this guy had just cursed at me in front of my daughter! In an instant, I wasn't in the Hamptons anymore, I was back on the streets of Queens and ready to teach him a lesson he wouldn't forget. "You're going to talk to me like that in front of my child?!" I screamed, rushing toward his car.

"That's a violation! Do you know what I should do to you?!" The second I started moving toward him, I could see the fear come over his face and I knew that I'd already gone too far. Yet I still couldn't stop myself, still couldn't find the strength and the courage to just accept what had happened, rather than respond to it.

Thankfully, before I was able to get to the guy, my friend stepped between us and held me back. Turning to the driver, he said, "Do yourself a favor and get out of here," and the guy was more than happy to comply, pulling off without saying another word.

After I'd calmed down, I was able to reflect on how I could have handled the situation with more grace and much less agitation. When the driver yelled at me, all I should have said was, "You're right, sorry for holding you up. Let me get out of your way." Not only because it had been rude for me to hold up traffic, but because instead of driving away, that guy could have stepped out of his car and kicked my ass up and down the street. Or shot me in the face. I had no idea who he was or what he was capable of. Worst of all, my daughter could have been needlessly hurt if something like that had gone down.

So while I obviously would have preferred that the driver hadn't cursed at me in front of my daughter, my reaction was worse for her to see than his words were for her to hear. What would have been more troubling to her? Hearing a stranger curse at her father? Or seeing that her father allowed that curse to throw him into a rage? Obviously the latter. If anything, by responding peacefully and graciously to those curses, I could have taught Ming Lee an important lesson in how to accept your mistakes and move on without getting entangled in them.

My hope is that my daughters—and all young people—will understand that there is always a different path they can take from the one that I chose that day. That one day Ming Lee or Aoki will be the woman whose response is "I'm sorry and I love you" if someone cusses *her* out in front of her child. I hope that she can understand that reacting with peacefulness and calmness in every situation doesn't make her a punk or weak or soft. Instead, I want her to see that the path of love is actually the most empowering one you can take through life.

If you're having trouble ditching the street mentality try this experiment. For one day, tell yourself that you're going to accept *everything* that the world throws your way. If someone cuts you while you're in line at the grocery store, don't say, "What do you think you're doing? Don't you see me standing here?" Just smile at him instead. If someone steps on your brand-new sneakers, don't get all worked up and start making threats. Just say, "No problem, it's all good." If someone is tailgating you on the freeway, just wave calmly instead of giving him the finger, or telling him to pull over so you can "settle" it. And, yes, if someone curses at you in front of your child because you're holding up traffic, then just say "I'm sorry" and walk away smiling.

Reacting to those kinds of situations with aggression might make you feel better for a moment, but I have to say it again, in the long run you're only wasting valuable energy. This is because someone cutting you in line, or tailgating you on the freeway expects you to yell at them. Mentally they've prepared for your aggression and have already built an emotional wall around themselves. So when your curse does come, it barely registers. You might as well be cursing into the wind. No matter how angry you get, it's not going to change that person's mentality.

On the flip side, if you greet their aggression with a sweet smile, or a friendly wave, you'll have a much better chance at breaking through their defenses. They won't be ready for the love you throw at them, and as a result, you might really get through to them. You might actually affect their behavior. Your love can make them reexamine their actions and words in a way that your hate never will.

MAKING YOURSELF SICK

If for some reason you're not concerned with the worldly implications of your angry, aggressive attitude, then consider this: Reacting to the world with a smile instead of a curse, a wave instead of the middle finger, will actually help you live longer.

You might not realize it, but every time you curse out a stranger, or get into a beef with someone you think dissed you, you're making yourself sick. That negative energy is going to pollute your body and literally take years off your life.

Not long ago a very close friend of mine was diagnosed with having precancerous cells under her tongue and was told to undergo surgery that would leave her unable to speak. Believing that there had to be a less invasive solution to her situation, I began taking her to meet various natural healers who might be able to suggest nonsurgical alternatives.

One of the first people we met with was the legendary author and nutritionist Gary Null. During the meeting, Gary shared his basic belief on well-being with us: Good health is made up of twenty-five percent diet, twenty-five percent exercise, and fifty percent happiness. In other words, staying happy and loving in your relationship with the world is more important to your health than any diet or workout plan you put yourself on.

Furthermore, Gary explained how angry, negative thoughts actually secrete inflammatory agents into our nervous systems, which in time manifest themselves into ailments like insomnia, high blood pressure, and even cancer. Conversely, loving, happy thoughts secrete anti-inflammatory agents, which will not only cure those ailments, but will prevent you from getting sick in the future. I don't mean to imply that everyone who contracts cancer or another illness is carrying hate in their hearts. Simone, for instance, is one of the most loving and caring people I've ever met.

But I do believe that while some illnesses are out of our hands, it is possible to make yourself sick with anger, hate, and regret. Thankfully, it's also possible to make yourself well with love and compassion. Those are qualities that will not only heal the world but heal whatever troubles you as well.

ACCEPTING YOUR RELATIONSHIPS

One area where it's particularly rewarding to adopt a happy, accepting mentality is your personal relationships. Our relationships with our families, close friends, and significant others are the ones where disappointment often stings the sharpest, loss lingers the longest, and betrayal cuts the deepest. Yet if you can learn to practice love unconditionally in those relationships, the pain will not only hurt less, but you'll be free to find the new love that's waiting for you out in the world.

Although I haven't evolved to the point where I can treat the entire world this way, I do practice unconditional love when it comes to my family. That doesn't mean we don't have our moments. Anyone who has seen me around my brothers or Kimora or even my nieces and nephews knows that it's not uncommon for me to raise my voice or drop a couple F-bombs. Yet despite any surface drama, my family members know that they can say anything to me (or do anything to me), and while

I might curse or complain about it for a moment, at the end of the day I'll still love and support them one hundred percent. Maybe one day as a family we'll progress to the point where we won't have to yell and argue, but for now, the important thing is that everyone accepts that the love between us doesn't have any limits or boundaries.

The presence of unconditional love has been a particular blessing in my relationship with Kimora. Even when our marriage was winding down, we managed to sidestep the hatred that poisons so many similar situations. Certainly we both felt moments of frustration, pain, and hurt, but we also worked very hard to move past those moments by accepting our relationship for what it was: two people who still loved and respected each other, but couldn't stay married any longer.

Through accepting that reality and then moving forward from it, most importantly we have been able to maintain a peaceful relationship when it comes to raising our daughters. Through accepting our breakup rather than being resentful of it, I've also been able to feel true happiness for Kimora's relationship with Djimon Hounsou and the birth of their son, Kenzo. And Kimora's acceptance of our divorce has allowed her to be supportive of my new relationships as well.

If either of us had been unable, or unwilling, to accept our breakup, we'd both be operating out of a much darker space right now. Our children, accustomed to seeing their parents fight, would be unhappy, no matter how much love we individually showered upon them. Without both of our visions and input, our joint business ventures like Simmons Jewelry would not do as well as they do today. And our relationship with the new people in our lives would suffer because of the residual drama from our battles over money, child-rearing, and the direction of our businesses.

Thankfully, none of that has been the case between Kimora and me. In fact, as we've started this new chapter in our relationship, my admiration and respect for Kimora has only increased. The world might know Kimora as many things: a fashion model, author, the genius behind Baby Phat, philanthropist, reality television star, talk-show host, *Top Model* judge . . . the list goes on and on. To me, she has been my partner, best friend, consultant, confidante, and the greatest mother for my daughters—she deserves all the credit for their manners, thoughtfulness, intelligence, kindness, and (I don't think anyone would disagree with this one) beauty.

There might be men who admire me for the amount of money I've made or the beautiful women I've been seen with on my arm. But, fellas, if you're going to sweat me for anything I've done, make it the relationship I've been able to maintain with Kimora. There are too many men out there who simply do not give their baby mommas the respect and love they deserve. If you've got children with an ex, look deep inside yourself and instead of appearing careless or resentful about the situation, try to acknowledge what a tremendous blessing that woman has been to your life. Accept that it is the dedication and commitment of that woman that allows you to go to sleep every night knowing that your children are safe and loved. Accept that it's her hard work that's teaching your children the tools and skills that they'll need to progress in this world. Even if there's drama over money or new relationships or your children's direction, accept that your ex is getting the job done when you can't or won't. And then celebrate her accordingly.

Finally, I want to promote a message of acceptance to all the single mothers who might be reading this as well. If your relationship with your children's father has run its course, try to accept it, even if you're still in love or not ready to let go. Or bitter that your man has moved on. I realize that can be one of the hardest things to do in life, but for your own sake, and the sake of your children, you must try to practice unconditional love. Even when that love isn't reciprocated, respected, or acknowledged.

If that seems beyond your present stage of evolution, it's OK. It's all a gradual practice. Instead, just try to focus on not hating that person. Because hating anyone, especially someone you used to love, is one of the greatest disservices you can do to yourself. I don't care if that person cheated on you, stole money from you, lied to you, or maybe even did all three. No matter what they did, you have to still love them unconditionally. If not for yourself, then for your kids. You want your children to be inspired by the power of love, and in order for them to do that, they need to see you exuding love in *all* situations, and to all people. Even the ones you might feel the most negatively toward.

Remember that experiment I just asked you to try with strangers who test you? To treat all those bad drivers and line cutters and sneaker scuffers with sweetness and gracefulness? Now try the same experiment with anyone you've become estranged from in your personal life. With the man who left you. With the woman who cheated on you. With the father who abandoned you. Or the child who disappointed you. Whatever happened, or whoever did it, look inside your heart and accept what's taken place without judgment or expectation. Accept that this person might not be the most attentive father, or the husband you'd hoped for, or even the most respectful child, but that you still love them anyway. And when you're able to love that way, you'll be radiating that attractive energy we spoke of earlier. You're already beautiful, but when you love everyone unconditionally, other loving people will see that and respond

to your energy. Your love will attract the man who is everything you've dreamed of, or the woman who makes you feel
whole. Just as love will mend even the most estranged relationships between a father and a son, or a mother and a daughter.

Loving unconditionally is always in your best interest. And
if you know that, but still find yourself struggling to find the
strength to love the world, then try to remember the words of
the Maharishi, who said, "There is no difficulty that enough
love will not conquer. No disease that enough love will not heal.
No door that enough love will not open. No gulf that enough
love will not bridge. No wall that enough love will not throw
down. No sin that enough love will not redeem. It makes no
difference how deeply seated may be the trouble, how great the
mistake. Sufficient realization of love will resolve it all. If only
you could love enough, you would be the happiest and most
powerful being in the world."

MOVING PAST WORRY

One of the greatest obstacles standing between us and our ability to accept the perfection of the world is anxiety. Back when
I had just started Def Jam, I used to spend many nights hanging
out in my office, sometimes even sleeping there. The outside
world pointed to that habit as a key to my success, evidence of
the hustle that separated me from less hungry and dedicated
executives.

While I didn't mind the competition believing I had an edge
on them, the truth wasn't that I was up all night working because I was more dedicated or relentless than anyone else: I was
there because my anxiety wouldn't let me fall asleep. I was worried about whether our albums were going to sell, whether my

partners were happy with me, or what my future in the business would hold. Rather than lie in my bed staring at the ceiling, I figured I might as well be at my desk trying to wring some value out of my anxiety. After a while though, I started to believe that my restless anxiety did actually have something to do with my success. I began to believe that without worry, I couldn't be focused. That without anxiety, I'd somehow lose my edge.

As I've written, initially I was even extremely apprehensive about yoga because it made me feel so peaceful. Coming out of yoga class and simply feeling happy in that moment—instead of worrying about what was around the next corner—was a shock to my system. I worried that I'd become so laid-back that I'd lose some of the "killer instinct" that was fueling my success. It took several practices before I was completely comfortable accepting that I actually functioned better and was much more effective without all that anxiety.

Now that I have been able to tap into that power of acceptance, I can see how wasteful I had been in the past. All the sleepless nights weren't getting me ahead; if anything they were holding me back. There was no value in worrying about a bunch of stuff I couldn't change. By holding on to my fears, I was only weighing myself down.

Nothing—not a lack of opportunity, or racism, or the economy, or haters—is more likely to derail your dreams than stressing over them. If you're a young hustler on the come up, you must have confidence that your hard work, dedication, and faith are going to pay off. You can't squander resources that you could be using today on worrying about tomorrow.

If you've already "made it," it's equally important that you let go of the anxiety that often accompanies success. I've seen too many people, many of them very close to me, let worry separate them from their gift. They might own several homes, drive a luxury car, and grace the cover of magazines, but they can't enjoy any of it. They're so consumed by anxiety that their mansion might as well be a shanty, and the magazine covers, "Most Wanted" posters. They are so nervous that it's all about to end that eventually it becomes a self-fulfilling prophecy. Anxiety is an equal opportunity destroyer. No matter who you are or what position you occupy, until you can purge anxiety from your life, any success and happiness you might enjoy will always be fleeting.

That's why one of the great ironies of my career is that while I did waste a lot of energy during those Def Jam days sweating the small stuff, I actually was not consumed with anxiety when faced with one of the biggest challenges of my days in the record business, which was my professional "breakup" with Rick Rubin.

When Rick and I founded Def Jam back in 1983, we shared a singular vision for the label: to promote the loud, uncut hip-hop we were hearing on the streets of New York City. But after we started selling a lot of albums and began to expand the label's scope, Rick and I found ourselves becoming interested in different things. Rick was becoming more passionate about producing hard-core rock acts like Slayer and Danzig, while I found myself increasingly drawn to working with R & B artists like Oran "Juice" Jones and Allison Williams. For a while we were able to find an acceptable balance for our dual visions, but eventually it became clear that our partnership was no longer as effective as it needed to be in order for Def Jam to thrive.

In the summer of 1988 Rick flew to New York (by that point he was spending almost all of his time in Los Angeles) so we could meet and figure out what to do once and for all. Sitting down for lunch at the NoHo Star, a restaurant near Def Jam's offices, we had a frank assessment of the situation. Without casting any blame, we agreed that as long as our visions were pulling us in opposite directions, all we'd end up accomplishing was stepping on each other's toes. Accepting that, Rick asked me if I wanted to leave the label. "Not really," I told him. "That's cool," he replied without rancor. "Then I'll leave." It was that simple. We decided that I would stay on at Def Jam and Rick would start his own label, which ultimately became Def American. We were both sad to be parting ways, but the meeting was remarkably free of anxiety. Rick wasn't worried that I was going to jerk him out of his monetary share of Def Jam and I wasn't worried that he was going to "steal" any of my acts. We didn't draw up any contracts, or bring in our lawyers to negotiate terms—we went on trust; we just agreed, as old friends who respected each other, to accept that we were no longer on the same page and move on.

It might sound like a logical decision on paper, but amicable breakups are actually extremely rare in the music industry, or in any industry for that matter. Normally when two people partner on an idea, experience success with it, and then have a difference of opinion on how to move it forward, the result is hurt feelings, resentment, and lawsuits. I've seen so many groups go to war with each other over the direction of their sound or image, with the ensuing battles inevitably leaving both sides irreparably harmed. By refusing to accept that a situation has run its course, or that people who used to see things the same way now view them differently, these artists end up destroying themselves and each other in a fruitless attempt to control something that is ultimately uncontrollable—creative vision.

I believe that one of the main reasons Rick and I have both been able to enjoy longevity in our careers is because we never fell prey to that sort of jealousy and resentment. By practicing acceptance, even in a situation where there was so much money on the table and emotional baggage under it, neither of us lost sleep over what couldn't be changed. Instead, Rick—who has been a longtime yogi—was able to apply all of his considerable talents to producing the artists that inspired him in Los Angeles, where he would go on to do groundbreaking work with the likes of The Red Hot Chili Peppers, Green Day, Metallica, and Johnny Cash. Meanwhile, I was freed up to be able to not only take Def Jam in a new direction, but also eventually launch new ventures like Phat Farm and *Def Poetry Jam*.

Most importantly, by accepting our situation for what it was, Rick and I have been able to remain great friends to this day. Our careers have taken us in different directions, but the bond that was forged so many years ago in an NYU dorm room remains unbroken. In 2009 VH1's *Hip-Hop Honors Awards* celebrated Def Jam's twenty-fifth anniversary and as part of the show, Rick and I filmed several clips in which we reminisced about the label's glory days. The clips caused something of a stir online and were hilariously lampooned by the comedian Affion Crockett. I can see why Affion had some fun at our expense— in the videos Rick talks about the Def Jam days while playing with his toes and fiddling with his prayer beads, while I do yoga stretches and stumble trying to recite some of my favorite Public Enemy rhymes. The two young lions of the 1980s had clearly transformed into middle-aged teddy bears. It was a transformation neither of us could have imagined twenty-five years earlier, but it was an undeniably beautiful one to me. A testament to the truth that sweetness, gracefulness, love, and acceptance will always win out in the long run.

MATERIAL BURDEN

*People surrounded by money but unable to use it
properly die of happiness thirst.*

— Paramahansa Yogananda

At this point in the book you've been introduced to numerous principles that will, to put it bluntly, help you make a lot of money. As we've discussed, the money and the toys will be a by-product of your ability to move through life as a sweet, humble, and generous giver.

Which is why I now need to remind all you happy, sweet, and generous givers one more time: While the money and the toys can be fun to play with, you must remember to never become attached to them. Otherwise, they will become a tremendous burden, significantly slowing down your journey toward enlightenment.

The yogis teach that "anything you cherish will make you sick," and I've certainly known many, many materially rich people who suffer from this affliction. They have become very sick, both emotionally and physically, through cherishing their toys. Their big houses and fancy cars might announce to the world that they "have it all," but in truth they are depressed and consumed with anxiety.

Theirs is an easily curable disease, yet they are so disconnected from their higher selves that they aren't even sensitive to what is making them so ill. They fail to see that the very things that the world is applauding them for—the money and the toys—are also the source of their suffering.

To be clear, the actual toys themselves are not the problem. One problem is that instead of inviting the world to share in their abundance, these individuals stockpile their possessions, hoping they will ensure their own happiness.

For instance, I know a guy who will happily spend two hundred thousand dollars flying a Victoria's Secret model all over the globe in an attempt (unsuccessful, I might add) to get laid, because he thinks that is what's supposed to make a rich middle-aged man happy. But he'll throw an absolute fit if you ask him to spend a fraction of that amount at a charity auction.

Just as I know another guy who will go out and buy two jets without blinking an eye, but if you ask him to write a ten-thousand-dollar check for charity, he'll look at you like you just asked for his left lung.

Despite having acquired so much of it, these individuals are completely unconscious of the value of money. They fail to realize that if money serves us any purpose in this life, it's solely to help alleviate suffering. Its value is not in building testaments to success, or even stashing it away in the bank for your children, because it will only make them sick too. The only real use for money is to help others become more comfortable in their seats. That's it. And if over time you are able to use your money to make enough people comfortable, then one day you'll find that you can be a little more comfortable in yours. Otherwise, as Yogananda puts it, you're going to "die of happiness thirst."

Because whether you realize it or not, you could own a house with a hundred seats in it, but if you're sitting in it all alone and don't invite others in to sit down and chill with you, you're never going to be happy. As I always say, "You can only sit your ass in one seat at a time." So if you're not sharing the rest of them with the world, all those other empty seats are just going to create a burden!

Though I know I can still do even better, I've tried to become more and more generous with the money and toys that have come into my life. I might not have reached the level of a Bill Gates or Warren Buffett yet, but I do run five charities and fund numerous political and social initiatives. And while I know I still could do better at giving, I've certainly never cried when someone's asked me to write a check for charity, or to help out with a cause. I know that if I ever start clinging to the money I've made, my own happiness is going to evaporate. As I wrote in *Do You!* my ultimate goal is to give away ninety-nine percent of what I make and live on the one percent that's left. And be happy doing it! To feel blissful and free every time I give away a dollar, instead of resentful and tight like so many rich folks.

There are so many burdens in life—disease, death, heartbreak, racism, poverty, and war—that truly are difficult to shed. The material burden is not one of them. So why add needlessly to your load? The truly enlightened person is going to enjoy playing with the toys the world throws at her feet, but she's certainly not going to want to hold on to them. She's not going to want to hold on to anything that's going to slow down her evolution, her journey of getting closer to God.

The enlightened ones know that true comfort only comes when you clear the noise out of your head. Worrying about how much your car is worth, or how much you spent to join an exclusive country club, or whether your friends have noticed your new fur coat will only add to that noise. Those kinds of thoughts promote confusion instead of clarity, distraction instead of serenity. The enlightened individual isn't interested in any of that: He is only interested in having a simple, happy, and uncluttered mind.

Again, I encourage you to enjoy all the toys that will inevitably come into your life when you follow these principles. As I said at the very beginning of the book, if your happy service happens to bring you a Rolls-Royce, then enjoy it! If it brings that HD TV, then have a blast watching all of your favorite movies on it! The point is that the value you place on those things should be very, very small. Yes, enjoy riding in the Rolls, but enjoy riding your bike just as much. You shouldn't feel bad about sitting on a nice couch, but you shouldn't mind sitting on a hard one either. In fact, you might actually like the hard one better!

None of us are so holy that we won't want to enjoy the toys for at least a few moments. I'm not asking anybody to deny himself or herself that sort of experience. I'm only asking you to move away from the belief that you need those toys to be happy, to be successful, to have "made it." Because nothing is further from the truth.

LOSING THE CONNECTION

In addition to never becoming attached to money and toys, we must also remember that one of our greatest sources of happiness is our gift of expression, not the toys that that expression might eventually attract. As we discussed earlier, our happiness lies in the process, never the results. Individuals in all walks of life struggle to remember this truth, but I've witnessed it as an especially difficult challenge for many rappers in particular.

The world might still stereotype rappers as violent, materialistic, or misogynistic, but I happen to know that the vast majority of them start off as very sweet kids—nerds, even—whose main focus in life is their desire to express their experience through poetry. They grow up watching the gangsters and hustlers who operated around them, but—and this is a very important distinction—very rarely did these poets get their own hands dirty. Instead, they retreated back to their rooms and wrote about the lifestyles they saw around them, rather than actually living a gangsta life themselves. They might have tried to sell a few bags of weed to buy some studio time or gone for a ride in a stolen car just to try to fit in, but if they did, they quickly realized that that life wasn't for them.

Because the characters and situations they wrote about were so authentic and filled with so much passion, the world fell in love with their poetry. Material successes followed and soon these young poets would find themselves in actual possession of the jewels and cars and clothes that before they could only fantasize about. Sadly, that intersection of fantasy and reality is also where the trouble would begin.

After signing their first record deal, almost every artist I knew would head to a car dealership and expect to find instant happiness in a new car. And they would find it, though only for a short period of time. I can't lie, the very first time you slide into the driver's seat of a brand-new luxury car, the reaction is, "Oh my God, would you look at this. The car smells like it just came out of a box, the seats feel like a sofa, and it rides the street like it has clouds for shock absorbers." But after you drive around the block a couple of times, slowly that "OMG" feeling starts to dissipate. It might happen after five rides, or it might take five thousand, but sooner or later that symbol of your arrival will reveal itself to be nothing more than a very intricate collection of metal and plastic parts. A very well-crafted collection, but ultimately nothing more or nothing less. That realization proves to be a tremendous letdown for these artists.

Unfortunately, when confronted with this truth, rather than turn back toward the source of their true inspiration—their poetry—the reaction of many artists is to load up even heavier on the toys. Just like the crackhead spends the rest of his life unsuccessfully chasing the rush from the very first time he gets high, these artists lose themselves chasing that fleeting feeling they got the first time they put on a fur coat, bought a diamond watch, or drove a luxury car.

In doing so, they begin to drift further and further away from their poetry and soon find themselves in places they weren't willing to go before. The nerds who were only comfortable watching the gangsters from out their window suddenly find themselves sitting next to those same gangsters in the club, popping champagne and getting high with them. Whereas before they would have run from the first hint of drama, now they court it. Because they've become separated from the root of their happiness, they begin to say reckless things that are out of character from them. Over time, these once peaceful, loving poets find themselves adrift in a sea of drama and posturing. And like any person swept out to sea, soon they're in danger of drowning.

When these artists look up and realize they've become lost at sea, instead of trying to head back to the shore, many simply lose their thirst for life. They give themselves over to the current and don't care if they ever make it back home or not. That might sound very dramatic, but I've witnessed it happen so many times. It's a very real phenomenon that will strike any artist (but this could just as easily apply to a lawyer or a doctor or businessperson) who confuses the toys with happiness. I could name a lot of famous names, but the example I'll share in detail is that of Rev Run, since he's already been very honest about the pain he went through when it happened to him.

Like the poets I just described, my brother grew up watching the gangsters and hustlers in our neighborhood, but Run and his partner, Darryl, were happiest when they were sitting in my parents' basement writing rhymes. The world loved their poetry and in a few years they were able to go from the basement to being the first hip-hop group to have an album hit number-one on the charts, see their videos played on MTV, land an endorsement deal, and even star in their own movies. During the mid-eighties they sold millions of albums and were largely responsible for introducing hip-hop to mainstream audiences. But instead of finding comfort in that worldly success, Run became overwhelmed by it.

After Run DMC helped tear down the walls holding back hip-hop, a whole new generation of rappers came pouring through the rubble. Poets that were hungry, starving even, for the type of success Run DMC had experienced. Today, Run can see that despite their hunger, those rappers had nothing but admiration and respect for him. To this day, in a culture built on competition and hubris, you've never heard a single rapper even slightly diss Run DMC or speak of them in anything less than reverential tones. At the time, however, Run was so disconnected from his gift that he couldn't feel any of that love. He was so isolated that he felt like those young rappers' only mission was to knock him off his position on top of the pile.

Instead of refocusing on his poetry, Run mistakenly believed that the way to stay on top was to look like he belonged there. So he blew millions on cars, Rolex watches, gold chains—any flashy toy he thought would make him look like the king of rap. He was able to ride that wave for a while, but eventually it caught up to him. The toys that were supposed to make him feel like a champion instead started making him feel very sick. As Run likes to caution young artists today, "When your world is all about consumption, in the end you're only going to consume yourself!"

As Run tells it, the realization that he had almost consumed himself finally hit him one day, while he was sitting in a hot tub. It was at the height of Run DMC's popularity and he was on tour, staying in one of the most expensive hotels in Los Angeles. Sitting in the tub, he had a plate of pancakes in one hand and a joint in the other while simultaneously getting his hair trimmed by his personal barber. He had just finished looking at a copy of the new *Rolling Stone* featuring a picture of Run DMC on the cover, the first rap group to ever receive that honor. It was the type of moment Run had dreamed about when he was growing up, being an artist on top of his game with every luxury at his fingertip.

Suddenly the phone next to the hot tub rang, and figuring it was a groupie he was expecting, Run lunged for it. In his haste, he accidentally ashed his joint onto his pancakes. He tried to brush the ashes off the pancakes, but only succeeded in knocking bits of hair into his syrup. He then tried to pick the hair out of the syrup, but since he was high, he ended up knocking the entire plate into the water. Looking down at his plate of soggy pancakes covered with hair and ash, he suddenly felt a wave of disgust and revulsion pass through his entire being. Not in response to the physical mess he'd created (though it did look nasty), but in response to how out of control his life had become.

Even though at that very moment he was one of the hottest artists in the country, Run had never felt so low in his life. Sitting in that hot tub staring at the mess he'd created, Run realized that he'd become completely disconnected from his gift. He might have had all the toys that he'd dreamed about back then, but he had none of the happiness. The Rolls-Royce, the *Rolling Stone* cover, the groupie, the weed, the hot tub—none of those things made him happy. Not because Rolls-Royces aren't fun to drive or hot tubs aren't relaxing to sit in, but because he had become attached to them. His entire existence was centered around how many toys he could juggle at once, how many excesses he could cram into one hotel suite. But when Run realized the toys he thought would make him a physical king had instead turned him into an emotional pauper, he actually thought about killing himself. His mind had become so cluttered by all the noise, and in his confusion he thought it would be easier to end his life than reacquaint himself with the things that really brought him joy and contentment.

Now here's the thing: If Run had been sitting in that tub smoking a joint, getting his hair cut, and eating pancakes while writing *a song*, he would have felt inspiration in that moment instead of despair. In fact, if he had been writing a song, he wouldn't have even been able to breathe, let alone do all those other things. Because when someone is locked in on being creative and sharing his gift, the world moves so slowly. He doesn't care about weed or groupies or even eating pancakes. He's completely focused on the work in front of him.

Instead, he was sitting in the hot tub worrying about record sales, what jewelry to buy, which car to ride in, which drugs to take, and which women to invite over—everything but his gift of music. And since that was certainly not the first time he'd been sitting in a hot tub focusing on worthless things, it was only a matter of time before that emptiness engulfed him.

Thankfully, instead of giving into the despair, Rev found the resolve to work his way back. He became involved in the Bishop Jordan's Zoe Ministries and committed to a spiritual process that allowed him to regain his love of life. Run had to accept that he already possessed everything that made him "the king," which in his case was his poetry. Whether that poetry expressed itself through rap, through his ministry, through *Run's House,* or even through his Tweets, it was never going to abandon him and it would always make him great.

Run's story, and the stories of so many other artists like him, hopefully will make you pause if you still think that you're going to find happiness in those toys. Your happiness is going to reside in your gift and your gift alone. Don't get so twisted that you feel like you're starting to drown before you straighten yourself out. The toys are ephemeral and hollow. Your gift is solid and lasts forever.

HAVING ENOUGH

One day during my most recent vacation in St. Bart's, my older daughter, Ming Lee, and I went shopping in order to find an art book that my younger daughter, Aoki, wanted for Christmas. I already had gotten Ming Lee a few gifts over the vacation, but since we were in the shopping district, I asked her if she wanted anything else.

"No, Daddy. Nothing I can think of," she said pleasantly.

"Nothing?" I asked, slightly surprised.

"I don't think so," she said. "I'd really just be happy if we could find this book for Aoki."

As a parent, it was a beautiful moment. Not many preteen girls, when told that their father is willing to break out the plastic, are more interested in finding something to make their sister smile than get something for themselves.

Which is not to say that she won't ever desire worldly things again. Ming Lee and Aoki might still be children, but trust me, they know a ten-thousand-dollar Birkin bag when they see one. Ming Lee might not want one of those bags today, but tomorrow it might seem like the most critical thing in the world. Despite maturity, I don't doubt that there will be plenty of clothes and jewelry and eventually even cars that she will feel like she needs in the years to come. But I'm very heartened that she's already started the journey toward at least lightening her load.

Some might suggest that the only reason Ming Lee said she didn't want anything else was because she's already received so much in her short life. And it's true: My kids have so many toys. I think they have every Ugly Doll or Hello Kitty bracelet ever made. But here's the thing: Collecting toys isn't like eating ice cream. At a certain point, we don't say, "Wow. I've had too much. I'm stuffed." Instead, whether we're rich or poor, young or old, black or white, we *always* think we need more. We're prepared to consume not only till we're stuffed, but until we're about to *die*. It's counterproductive, but it's our nature. That's why our goal should be to fight past that instinct and realize that instead of needing everything, we actually need *nothing*.

I've read that when Gandhi died, all of his worldly possessions could be counted on two hands: a pair of dinner bowls, a wooden fork and spoon, his diary, a prayer book, a watch, a spittoon, a letter opener, and a set of porcelain monkeys acting out the "see no evil/hear no evil/speak no evil" motif. That's it. He was one of the most influential men in the entire world, but those were the only things he owned.

Gandhi kept it so simple because as a highly enlightened individual, he wasn't interested in chasing worldly things. He understood that the goal is to have your thoughts, actions, and words coming from a higher state of consciousness where we attain a state of needing nothing.

To all of you who think this talk about "needing nothing" seems unrealistic, or idealistic, in the face of the world's realities, do me a favor: Ask yourself what you need this very second. Right now.

You probably couldn't think of anything, could you?

That's because in this second, right now, you truly don't need anything. Sure, if I gave you ten seconds, you could probably come up with a couple of things you feel like you need. More money, a new car, or better health insurance.

If I gave you an hour, you could probably write me a whole book about what you need (though an hour from now you *still* won't need anything!). But in this second, there's nothing you need so greatly that it stands out above everything else. Gandhi understood that and as a result he was able to walk through life unburdened. He lived by the Sanskrit prayer: *Lokah samastah sukhino bhavantu.* Or, "May all beings know peace, and may my thoughts, words, and actions contribute in some way to that peace."

The state that Gandhi lived and died in is the one we all want to be moving toward. Having said that, I don't think many people picked up this book because they wanted to live like Gandhi. As inspiring as he was, you're probably not ready to make that sort of commitment. Which is why I'm not telling anyone they need to give it all away. I'm not telling you to trade in your Manolo Blahniks for a pair of dusty old sandals, or your fine china for a wooden fork and spoon. Besides, even if you were prepared to make those trades, I'd still encourage you to make them carefully, because it's not healthy to suddenly leap out of the world like that. Instead, slowly, at your own pace, simply begin to find a better balance with the toys. To enjoy your possessions without being consumed by them. You can be moving in the right direction without being a saint. And in the meantime be grateful for all the things you do have, not the toys but your health, your family, your friends, a roof over your head, your sanity—whatever it might be.

NOT TOO HOLY

*My imperfections and failures are as much
a blessing from God as my successes and my talents
and I lay them both at his feet.*

—GANDHI

Let us return, for a final time, to the conversation between Lord Krishna and Arjuna on the battlefield.

In particular, the moment when Arjuna finally overcame his misgivings about Lord Krishna's instructions and realized that he had been blessed with an amazing gift of wisdom and insight.

Despite having come to the battlefield timid and unsure, Arjuna awoke from his slumber and began to feel very confident about his purpose. So much so that he decided that rather than learn only from his teacher's human avatar, he was ready to experience Lord Krishna's ultimate self. In other words, Arjuna was ready to immerse himself in pure holiness.

"I really love listening to you," he then told Krishna. "But it seems that I still don't know your ultimate self. If it's not too much of a hassle, I'd appreciate it if now you could reveal that self to me."

"Are you sure?" responded Lord Krishna. "My divine form might be more than your human eyes can see, or your human mind can comprehend."

"Don't worry, teacher, I'm ready," replied Arjuna. "I'm feeling very devout right now, so I want to soak in every last drop of your truth and power. I know that if I can fully comprehend your being, then I'll be the baddest dude on this battlefield."

"I'm not sure this is the right move," said Lord Krishna. "But since you're my man, I will reveal my total self to you. So get ready."

And with those words, Lord Krishna was no longer a humble charioteer, but instead began to change forms by the millisecond. In rapid succession he went from appearing as a beautiful baby to the rotting corpse of an old man to a tender lover to a coldhearted murderer to a loving father bouncing Arjuna on his knee to a hideous monster eating Arjuna and his family alive. Then he appeared as a sublime sunset, followed by a terrible hurricane. And as he shifted shapes, he went from singing the loveliest melody ever heard by human ears to screaming like a lamb caught in a lion's jaws. Lord Krishna's ultimate self was at once a beautiful and terrifying thing to behold.

Arjuna tried to watch, but after even just a few moments he felt himself starting to go crazy from all the intense images he was seeing. "Lord Krishna, please make it stop!" he finally begged. "I thought I could handle your truth, but you're on a whole different level, one I can't even begin to comprehend. Please forgive me, because I obviously didn't have any business asking to witness your divine form."

"Don't worry, it's all good," said Lord Krishna, returning, much to Arjuna's relief, to the form of a charioteer. "It's only natural that you were frightened. You'd have to be extremely enlightened to be able to smile at a corpse the same way you would smile at a baby. To treat those two objects the same would require an unshakeable belief that the world is in perfect order. Even though you're a good dude, you're not quite there yet.

"That's why I need you to understand that until that day comes, don't get caught up in trying to be perfectly enlightened. Don't stress being quite so holy," continued Lord Krishna. "Just stay focused on chanting my name in meditation and spreading love through your work. If you can do that, you'll be moving closer to me."

I wanted to share that story because it's a particularly appropriate note to sound at the end of this book. While it would be fantastic if everyone could effortlessly become enlightened, that probably won't be the case. Just as it was impossible for Arjuna to stare at Lord Krishna in his entirety without years of preparation and practice, it would prove impossible for you to wake up tomorrow and adopt the principles of this book in their entirety as well.

That's certainly not to compare my humble advice to Lord Krishna's timeless teachings, but rather to comment on the general nature of spiritual evolution: There will always be some contradiction between the divinity in our hearts and what we are able to actually practice in the world.

This is true even in the extreme case of someone like Mother Teresa, a literal saint who was one of the most inspirational figures of the last century, no matter what your faith. Yet despite Mother Teresa's unquestioned enlightenment, her diaries reveal that even she struggled over whether she was holy enough. She certainly wasn't getting high, chasing money, or being promiscuous, but she definitely questioned her relationship with God. She wrote that because "I was forever smiling," people thought "my faith, my hope, and my love are overflowing, and that my intimacy with God and my union with his will fill my heart. If they only knew. . . . In my own heart, I feel the terrible pain of [the loss of God]. I feel that God does not want me, that God is not God and he does not really exist."

Mother Teresa was probably one of the holiest people to walk the Earth during our lifetimes, but even she felt she wasn't holy enough. That's why the next time you're feeling off track, don't forget that even someone with such an intimate relationship with God as Mother Teresa had a glimpse of the same kind of doubt and pain as you might.

THE TWO Cs

If you were to isolate a single concept in this book that you could not only carry through life, but perhaps share with your friends as well, I would hope that it would be what I call the "Two Cs": consciousness and compassion.

Whether you're a yogi, Muslim, Hindu, Christian, Jew, or don't believe in God at all, if you make a real commitment to being conscious and compassionate, it's inevitable that you'll receive the lasting happiness that all of us are searching for. Even if you fall short in all the other areas we've discussed, as long as you're focused on being awake and kind, it will be impossible for you to stray too far off the righteous path.

That's why every day you should set the simple goal of trying to be more awake and less distracted. As I've said, you can increase your awareness through meditation, prayer, yoga, listening to music, painting, reading, and getting lost in your work—any activity that helps you shut out the noise and become a little better reacquainted with your higher self. And while you should still love those who suffer from delusion or unconscious behavior, don't spend too much time around them. Their unconsciousness can be extremely contagious. When you see those types, just give them a pound and then keep it moving! You want to make sure everyone in your inner circle is conscious and awake, striving to reach the same enlightenment that you are. Or as I like to post on Twitter from time to time, "Hang with people who lift u up. Separate from those who take u down."

Being awake is going to be central to all your success. Everything of quality that you accomplish in your outer, or worldly, life will stem from your inner life. Conversely, if all your energy is focused on your outer life—on making money, collecting toys. and experiencing worldly success—it's going to be very hard to slow down that momentum and turn back inward when you inevitably realize the trophies you've collected have no real value.

To offer you an analogy, basketball coaches always stress having a strong "inside-out game." What those coaches mean is if their team can first establish its "inside game" (or taking shots close to the basket), then it will have a much easier time with its "outside game" (or shots taken far away from the basket). It's one of the basic laws of basketball—when you work on becoming strong on the inside first, that success will open up the rest of your game.

Try to "play" your life the same way! When you use meditation, yoga, or prayer to build up that strong "inside" (consciousness) game, then the points (or worldly success) will come so much easier. Whether it's basketball or life, when your strength emanates from the inside, you can't help but win.

But while the world's successes will be nice, the best part of having that strong "inside game" is that it will allow you to actually leave the world for brief moments during which you can catch a glimpse of God. "Catching a glimpse" might at first seem like a fairly pedestrian goal, but as Arjuna's reaction to Lord Krishna's ultimate self reminds us, when we first set out on the road toward enlightenment, we can't really handle more than a glimpse anyway.

The longer you can remain committed to practices that promote consciousness, then in time those glimpses will begin to last longer and longer. Until what started off as a fleeting glimpse becomes a long, peaceful gaze. And when you're able to gaze at the God inside you, then you will be The Watcher. Then you will be living in a state of grace. Then you will be a miracle worker. Then you will have truly "won" the game of life. As the yogis say about those who have reached enlightenment, "there will be no coming back for you. You've reached the end of suffering."

The second "C" is compassion. In the classical study of yoga there are five *yamas* (or "restraints") that compose the code of conduct by which all conscious human beings are expected to live. The first (and consequently, most important) of these *yamas* is "*Ahimsa*," which means living in a compassionate and non-harming manner.

This unfailing belief in compassion, both in thought and action, must become the soundtrack to your life. No matter how jealous, covetous, angry, or desperate you become, the moment you even think about harming someone or something else, your mind must sound an *Ahimsa* alarm. A wake-up call to remind you that you must make a more compassionate choice.

Learning how to make the compassionate choice in any and all situations would be such a beautiful skill to take from this book. That's because if you can truly live in accordance to *Ahimsa*, then all other principles we've discussed will have no choice but to fall into place.

Of course, living a completely compassionate life is easier said than done. While most everyone agrees that actions like murder, rape, and torture are unacceptable, we have a more difficult time identifying the more subtle forms of harmful behavior.

I am realizing that in order to truly practice *Ahimsa*, a person must be prepared to reevaluate all of their actions, even the ones that seem so far removed from any type of exploitation or harmfulness. And while I'm not telling you that there's anything inherently wrong with making money, I am saying that your profit should never be connected in any way to exploitation or abuse. Just as while I'm not admonishing you for driving a fly SUV, I am reminding you that the more you participate in the exploitation of Mother Earth, the less you'll be able to appreciate all of her true riches.

HAPPINESS AND FREEDOM FOR ALL

Perhaps the most popular mantra among American yogis is that Sanskrit phrase I shared earlier, *Lokah samastah sukhino bhavantu*, "May beings everywhere be happy and free. And may the thoughts, actions, and words of my own life somehow contribute to that happiness and to that freedom for all." And really, that's the message of the Two Cs in a nutshell. To walk through life promoting happiness and freedom for everyone, not just those who look like you, talk like you, dress like you, or pray like you. To not only promote that universal freedom, but to be conscious enough in your actions tò make sure you're contributing to it as well. And perhaps most importantly, to have fun doing it. As the Maharishi says, "Nothing in life has to be taken seriously—except the joy of life."

Having now reminded you a final time of the power of consciousness and compassion, I'd like to end this book by quoting, appropriately enough, Arjuna's final words in the Bhagavad Gita.

"Through your kind conversation, I've woken up and am conscious of who I really am," Arjuna tells Lord Krishna. "And now that I have your instructions, I'm not nervous or fearful anymore. Instead, I'm ready to get out there and fight!"

Hopefully this book, though admittedly vastly inferior in all forms, will have inspired you in the same way that Lord Krishna inspired Arjuna.

And like Arjuna, I hope you have found a few words in these pages that have helped you awaken from your slumber and served to reacquaint you with the inextinguishable light of God inside of you.

And once again like Arjuna, now that you're armed with that knowledge, you're ready to go out into the world and fight.

To fight not for what you can get for yourself, but what you can give to others.

To fight not for your own abundance, but for the abundance of others.

To fight not for your own security, but for the peace and safety of others.

To fight not for your own joy, but for the happiness of others.

To fight not for your own upliftment, but for the enlightenment of others.

When you are devoted to fighting for these things with a smile on your face and love radiating out of your heart, then all these things will be yours.

You will have it all.

You will be Super Rich.